IMAGES
of America

ASHEVILLE'S
ALBEMARLE PARK

THE LODGE. The Lodge, or gatehouse, constructed in 1898, was the first structure in Albemarle Park. With its graceful arch and massive stone-and-shingle-wrapped tower, characteristic of the Shingle style, it presented a welcoming gateway to the quintessential English-themed inn envisioned by the designers. The Lodge originally served as both a residence and office for the inn. Thomas Raoul lived here until moving into Manzanita Cottage in 1906. (RSSR.)

ON THE COVER: THE MANOR AND COTTAGES OF ALBEMARLE PARK. This picturesque community, evocative of Asheville's dramatic turn-of-the-century resort town boom era, was the artful creation of Thomas Wadley Raoul and his father, William Greene Raoul, whose collaboration with Bradford Gilbert and Samuel Parsons resulted in one of the nation's earliest planned residential parks. (RFP, Emory.)

IMAGES
of America

ASHEVILLE'S
ALBEMARLE PARK

Stacy A. Merten and Robert O. Sauer

ARCADIA
PUBLISHING

Copyright © 2014 by Stacy A. Merten and Robert O. Sauer
ISBN 978-1-5316-7289-8

Published by Arcadia Publishing
Charleston, South Carolina

Library of Congress Control Number: 2013946735

For all general information, please contact Arcadia Publishing:
Telephone 843-853-2070
Fax 843-853-0044
E-mail sales@arcadiapublishing.com
For customer service and orders:
Toll-Free 1-888-313-2665

Visit us on the Internet at www.arcadiapublishing.com

We dedicate this work to all of the individuals and
institutions who have acted as stewards of Albemarle Park
through the preservation of its architecture, landscape,
and archival material that made this effort possible.

CONTENTS

ACKNOWLEDGMENTS

This book has been both a joy and a challenge as we have endeavored to overcome the obstacles of finding our collective voice, setting boundaries, and distilling the essence of vast research into a brief synopsis with the intention of conveying the spirit of Albemarle Park to a new generation of sojourners.

We would like to thank the following people who have assisted us with this project: Jane G. and Richard A. Mathews for their preservation work in Albemarle Park and *The Manor and Cottages*; Albemarle Park Manor Grounds Association; Scott Riviere for his perpetual optimism and preservation integrity; Zoe Rhine for her expertise; Martha Fullington for editing; Peggy Gardner for her succor; Christy Edwards for Photoshop assistance; Patty McFarland for moral support; Brian Estes for his encouragement; Cathy Ball, Judy Daniel, and members of the Historic Resources Commission for their backing and support; Bill Alexander for sharing Biltmore Estate documents; the librarians at Emory who endured our excited whisperings as we reviewed the Raoul archives; Margaret Sandresky and Dr. Crys Armbrust for Nina Simone's history; Jack Thomson with the Preservation Society of Asheville and Buncombe County; and Allison Dennis with the Town of Biltmore Forest.

Unless otherwise noted, the images used in this book are identified at the end of each caption based on the key that follows: photographs courtesy of Raoul Family Papers and Jane Raoul Bingham Papers, Manuscripts, Archives, and Rare Book Library, Emory University (RFP, Emory) and (JRBP, Emory); North Carolina Collection, Pack Memorial Public Library, Asheville, North Carolina (NCC, Pack); E.M. Ball Photographic Collection and Holladay Collection of John B. Robinson Photographs, D. Hiden Ramsey Library, Special Collections, University of North Carolina Asheville (EMB, Ramsey) and (HCJBRP, Ramsey); Manor Inn Photographic Collection, Western Regional Archives, State Archives of North Carolina (State Archives); Nina Simone Memorial Project (NSP); Albemarle Park Manor Grounds Association (APMGA); Library of Congress (LOC); Collection of Robert Sauer and Scott Riviere (RSSR); the personal collection of Fred Kahn (FK); Tennessee State Library and Archives Photographic Collection (TSLA); the Town of Biltmore Forest (BF); and the Preservation Society of Asheville and Buncombe County (PS).

INTRODUCTION

Albemarle Park is a small community located on Charlotte Street, tucked away at the base of the western slope of Sunset Mountain. While many in Asheville are likely familiar with The Manor, prominently sited on a knoll overlooking Charlotte Street, or the Lodge (gatehouse), stately marking the entrance to the neighborhood, they may not be as familiar with the community itself or its fascinating history. Also known as The Manor and Cottages, the development was the unique intention of the Raoul family to differentiate their endeavor from the typical hotel or boardinghouse common to Asheville's boomtown-era expansion that followed in the wake of the industrial revolution.

Asheville's Albemarle Park tells the story of the Raoul family and the early development of the community through an assembly of historical images and ephemera, collected from a variety of sources. The intention is to convey the history of the development while revealing the spirit of the time and place and the inspiration guiding the vision of the people who shaped the natural environment through thoughtful planning, architecture, and landscape design. In an increasingly globalized and rapidly changing world, the concept of finding meaning or identity through connection to place has become ever more relevant to psychological well-being. Although once seen as distinctly separate, man and nature are now perceived as related, each influencing the other through time. The landscape, where man and nature come together, can be read as a document of human history, replete with many layers of time and human values, creating a palimpsest informing the genius of a place. Thomas Wolfe, whose figure reoccurs throughout the story as a local personality of national literary importance, was also someone who deeply understood and was able to capture in a most eloquent fashion the importance of place in his work.

The Raouls purchased the land that was to become Albemarle Park in 1886 with the intention of building a summer home, but those plans were put on hold after William Greene Raoul lost his position with the Central Railroad of Georgia over a stock battle and moved his family to New York. The property lay dormant for a decade until Thomas Wadley Raoul, the son of William Greene, was diagnosed with tuberculosis at the age of 21. Tuberculosis was the leading cause of death in the United States at the time, and although it flourished in urban areas, it was relatively uncommon in mountainous areas of the United States and Europe. Asheville offered the best combination of altitude, atmosphere, and climate considered essential to the treatment of the lung disease. The leading pulmonary specialists and physicians of the time were attracted to Asheville, where they developed facilities for research and treatment of the disease. Thomas returned to Asheville for his health and soon began clearing land at the "Asheville Place." Although development of a boardinghouse was not the original plan, Thomas and his father eventually warmed to the idea. In seeking a dignified name for the project, they settled on Albemarle Park, in reference to the Duke of Albemarle, who had held the original grant from King Charles II of England to the land that later became North Carolina.

The Raouls had an obvious appreciation of the natural world, reflected in their writings, activities, and interests, as well as their predominant use of Shingle-style elements in the architecture of Albemarle Park. The Shingle style, with its roots in the Queen Anne and Colonial styles, eventually emerged as the first truly American style of architecture. Characterized by its rambling form, extending the house into the landscape, it was described by Vincent J. Scully Jr., Sterling Professor at Yale University, as "the picturesque desire to be close to nature." In addition to the extensive use of wooden shingles, the style typically incorporates massive stone foundations emerging from the ground, attempting to evoke the surrounding landscape and site characteristics within a regional context. Wraparound porches, terraces, and towers are widely used, providing various options for interaction with the outdoors and the integration of interior spaces with the site and setting. Interiors are informal and oriented to celebrate landscape vistas. The style, best suited for country or suburban settings, was predominantly used for summer homes and resorts, with the use of deep porches and overhangs allowing the homes to be livable while withstanding more extreme weather conditions. The Rustic Shingle style became popular with the National Park Service for lodgings and caretaker cottages.

The emergence of a few characters in the story, including Thomas Raoul himself, point to the overlap between the popularity of the Shingle style and the formative period of American environmentalism. An early promoter of the national parks, Theodore Roosevelt, whose conservation policies were intertwined with the Country Life Movement, joins Dr. Chase Ambler for a brief appearance. Ambler, a pulmonary specialist, was an early advocate of the Weeks Act, which allowed the use of federal funding for the purchase of forest land, thus advancing the formation of the United States Forest Service.

William Greene Raoul never expected Albemarle Park to turn a profit, although the sale in 1920 to Edwin Wiley Grove netted over half a million dollars; for Raoul, it was an opportunity to design, create, and express his artistic urges. Mary Raoul Millis, the daughter of William Greene, wrote in her memoir, *The Family of Raoul*, "Let me affirm that our Parents were both exceptional people; each outstanding, each strong in his own right, each a vivid, dramatic figure, impressing his personality upon his environment."

The Manor and Cottages of Albemarle Park received the honor of listing in the National Register of Historic Places in 1977, described in the nomination as a community composing a highly picturesque district with a mix of architectural styles, incorporating elements of the Shingle, half-timbered Tudor, and gambrel-roofed Colonial Revival that also represents a significant historic landscape and a rare intact example of early residential community planning in the United States. But it is not merely an artifact. While the early development of the community echoes the social, political, and cultural attitudes of its time, united with the natural conditions of the region, retaining a high degree of integrity and conveying the feeling of a bygone era, it also thrives today as living, breathing community, conveying a strong sense of place that continues to evolve, shaped by the people who now call it home.

"A stone, a leaf, an unfound door. Where? When? O lost, and by the wind grieved, ghost, come back again," reads Thomas Clayton Wolfe's *Look Homeward, Angel*. Like the poetic opening to Wolfe's novel, we invite you to reminisce for a while. Sit back, relax, and absorb these images of a time gone by. Indulge your imagination as you contemplate the options of spending the season in Chipmunk or Clover and experience a brief glimpse of Albemarle Park, a place that in many ways embodies a certain graciousness and charm that endures as the essence of Asheville.

One

A TIME AND A PLACE

Tourism in Asheville was first promoted in 1876 when Christian Reid published a book titled *Land of the Sky*. Her book painted a romantic vision of Asheville as an ideal summer resort on par with Saratoga, New York. Her target audience included tourists flocking to the mountains in escape of the oppressive southern summer heat and invalids from around the country seeking the therapeutic benefits offered by the region's climate, believed at the time to be beneficial for patients suffering from tuberculosis. But it was the long anticipated arrival of the railway into Asheville in 1880 that solidified Western North Carolina as a tourist destination and changed the region forever.

The railroad also brought Gilded Age capitalists and entrepreneurs eager to make a profit. One of them, Col. Franklin Coxe, who grew up in the foothill region of North Carolina, was responsible for the construction of Asheville's premiere Victorian-era hotel, the Battery Park Hotel. Set atop what was then known as Battery Porter Hill in downtown Asheville, it was described by Thomas Wolfe as "a vast new hotel, a sumptuous wooden barn, rambling comfortably upon the summit of a commanding hill." Other such hotels, inns, and boardinghouses, including Wolfe's mother's place on Spruce Street, now a National Historic Landmark, were commonplace.

This was the Asheville to which William Greene Raoul arrived with his wife, Mary Wadley Raoul, and their growing family to spend their first summer in 1886. During their stay at an Asheville boardinghouse, Mary took the children for a walk one day out to a small farm on Charlotte Street, where they stopped to get some milk. As they sat by the springhouse drinking milk and feeding fish in a nearby pond, it occurred to Mary that the place would make an ideal summer home. Consequently, the Raouls purchased about 42 acres from a Mr. Deaver and converted his small farmhouse for use as a temporary residence while the family decided on the style and location of their permanent home.

ASHEVILLE LOOKING SOUTHWEST ACROSS FRENCH BROAD RIVER VALLEY. This panorama, taken near Beaucatcher Mountain, depicts Asheville much as the Raoul family would have first experienced it in 1886. The Battery Park Hotel is visible atop Battery Porter Hill at upper right, and the old county courthouse dome appears in the upper left. The Blue Ridge Mountains, with Mount Pisgah prominent, grace the horizon. (NCC, Pack.)

ASHEVILLE COUNTRYSIDE. The Asheville countryside in the late 19th century, with its patchwork of fields and forests, was a summer resort for many escaping the southern heat. Mary Raoul, captivated with the countryside, convinced her husband, William, to purchase a small tract of land in 1886 from the Deaver Farm on Charlotte Street. Initially, the Raouls planned to live in the existing farmhouse while making plans for their permanent home. (NCC, Pack.)

Southern Railroad Depot, Asheville, N. C.

SOUTHERN RAILWAY STATION. With the arrival of the railroad in 1880, the population of Asheville exploded, nearly quadrupling by 1890. The railway station in the village of Best, now Biltmore Village, was the site of the original passenger depot in Asheville. This Spanish Mission–style station served as an Asheville gateway for many years, in operation from 1904 to 1968, when it was demolished. (NCC, Pack.)

ORIGINAL BATTERY PARK HOTEL, 1902. Designed and built by John Adam Wagner, the rambling Queen Anne–style structure situated on 25 acres with magnificent mountain views was owned and operated by Col. Frank Coxe, a pioneer of the railroad era who invested private funds to help bring the railroad to Asheville. The hotel, which opened in 1886, largely established Asheville as a tourist destination. (NCC, Pack.)

PLEASURE PARTY AT THE BATTERY PARK HOTEL, AROUND 1900. Colonel Coxe prepares for a ritual excursion into the countryside with hotel guests seated aboard his four-in-hand pleasure coach *Maude*. Colonel Coxe suggested the idea of creating a boardinghouse with Thomas Raoul and his father while relaxing on the hotel's porch during one of their stays. (NCC, Pack.)

THE OLD KENTUCKY HOME, 1908. Thomas Wolfe, who immortalized Asheville in his novel *Look Homeward, Angel*, sits on a wall with his family in front of his boyhood home, a boardinghouse run by his mother, Julia. Wolfe wrote of the house: "Dixieland. . . . It was situated five minutes from the public square on a pleasant middle-class street of small homes and boardinghouses. It had a pleasant front yard, not deep but wide, bordered by a row of young deep-bodied maples." (NCC, Pack.)

Two

THE CIRCLE

OF THE FOUNDERS

William Greene Raoul, and his wife, Mary Wadley Raoul, set the development of Albemarle Park in motion. An influential railroad magnate, Raoul was well traveled, sophisticated, and possessed keen eyes and skilled hands. The Raouls' daughter Mary Raoul Millis wrote, "Beauty delighted his soul—especially beauty of line and form; the beauty of fine craftsmanship, and the harmony of good design."

Two key New York designers were hired to plan Albemarle Park: Bradford Gilbert, Raoul's friend and architect, and Samuel Parsons Jr., landscape architect. Gilbert was a friend with whom Raoul had developed a good working relationship while designing railroad stations, residences, and other projects. Thomas Raoul described The Manor's planning: "He and Mr. Gilbert were sitting at a dinner table opposite each other, and Father was illustrating with his hands, as he so often did, showing in which direction was the mountain view, when Mr. Gilbert said, 'I have it! We will build the house just as you sit'—and so they did." Samuel Parsons Jr. brought respect for the natural landscape and excellent design experience of public parks. The manorial Biltmore Village was begun in 1895, and a few planned communities were established around the eastern states. Albemarle Park was one of those early residential parks, presenting one of the most challenging sites. The Raoul family of 12 had a wide sphere of influence, and their spouses would later add further that sphere. Each forward-thinking individual brought his or her own talents, knowledge, and expertise to the project and that combined to create a unique residential park.

WILLIAM GREENE RAOUL. At age 18, Raoul served in the Civil War, becoming a captain in charge of the Confederate Railway Bureau's car construction and transportation of Army supplies. Later, he became an executive in several railroad companies, including president of the Mexican National Railroad. Other accomplishments included the invention of the air brake and starting a foundation for the eradication of tuberculosis. However, as his daughter Mary wrote, "The story of Albemarle Park shows Father in the role he loved the best. Dynamic executive though he was, these other parts he loved to play were nearer to his heart, and more truly expressive of his inmost character. To design, to create, to express Beauty and Order—this was his fundamental urge . . . the project provided not only relaxation from arduous labor, not only a charming second home for his family, not only congenial occupation for his beloved son, Tom, but afforded him a superlative medium of self-expression." (RFP, Emory.)

MEXICAN NATIONAL RAILROAD COMPANY. After purchasing the Deaver Farm in Asheville, Raoul became president of the Mexican National Railway from 1887 to 1904, with his office in New York City. He had been president of the Central Railroad and Banking Company and various associated lines, including the Ocean Steamship Company, Atlantic & Birmingham Railway, and the Southwestern Railroad. Links between Mexico, New York, Georgia, and Asheville were via Raoul's private railcar, which included a cook. (LOC, LC-D418-30155.)

MARY WADLEY RAOUL. The daughter of railroad executive William Wadley, Mary lived in Savannah and near New Orleans prior to her marriage. After marrying Raoul, she became a mother of 10. She helped promote the Free Kindergarten movement, helped found the Equal Suffrage Party of Georgia in 1914, served on the board of the Cotton States and International Exposition, and was a member of the Every Saturday Club, Daughters of the American Revolution, and the Daughters of the Confederacy. (RFP, Emory.)

708 PEACHTREE STREET HOUSE INTERIOR, AROUND 1891. Bradford Gilbert designed the rose brick and shingled Raoul family home that stood three stories tall on fashionable Peachtree Street in Atlanta. He designed the interior woodwork enriched with hand carvings as well as furniture for the entrance hall with the same carvings. Loring Raoul remembered the wet plaster being "checkerboarded" with a comb; this photograph shows it with a basket weave pattern. (RFP, Emory.)

YOUNG RAOUL BROTHERS. This studio composition photograph shows, from left to right, Loring, William, Norman, Gaston, and Thomas (on the floor). Mary wrote of their father, William Greene Raoul, "He loved to take his little boys with him into the railroad shops and yards, and for short trips in his official car. He always explained things to us—how things were done, and what made the wheels go round." (RFP, Emory.)

SAMUEL PARSONS JR., LANDSCAPE ARCHITECT. Parsons, a third-generation Quaker horticulturist, first worked with his trailblazing plant-importer father, who saw gardening as an art form like painting or sculpture. They grew native plants and were first to propagate rhododendrons in the United States. Parsons Jr. studied agricultural chemistry and philosophy at Yale, then followed his inclination for landscape design by joining Calvert Vaux's firm. Their designs would preserve the best elements that nature had given to a site. Parsons later became the superintendent of Central Park and then head landscape architect for the City of New York. Author of magazine articles and several books, he advocated the values of the romantic tradition in landscape design. He acquired proficiency with steep slopes while working on Riverside and Morningside (below) Parks, which proved useful in the design of Albemarle Park. (Right, National Cyclopaedia; below, RSSR.)

St. Luke's Hospital and Morningside Park, New York.

BRADFORD LEE GILBERT, ARCHITECT. Gilbert's architectural practice (above) was in Manhattan, where he designed structures throughout North America. Gilbert was named "the father of the skyscraper" for designing the Tower Building in 1888. He was employed by 18 railroad companies; one commission included the Laconia, New Hampshire, passenger station (below). Other projects included international expositions, clubs and public buildings, residences, and books on his architecture. Many designs were in a Romanesque Revival style, which used colored bricks—reds and oranges—with patterns set into colored masonry. The Raoul buildings in Asheville and Atlanta were in the Shingle style; their arches, towers, and colored mortars were Gilbert's signatures. (Above, Dickinson College, Archives and Special Collections; below, RSSR.)

R. R. Station, Laconia, N. H.

FLATIRON BUILDING, ATLANTA. Albemarle Park was not Gilbert's first challenging site. Following his 11 or 13-story Tower Building constructed on a narrow 21-foot-wide lot, he designed this English-American Building, later known as the Flatiron Building. Constructed in 1897 on Peachtree Street, it predates New York's famous Flatiron Building by five years and remains the oldest steel-framed high rise in Atlanta. (RSSR.)

COTTON STATES AND INTERNATIONAL EXPOSITION, 1895. Prior to designing Albemarle Park, Bradford Gilbert worked as the supervising architect of the exposition to showcase American technology and products and to foster trade to South America. Gilbert designed most of the complex of buildings sited in what would become Piedmont Park. (LOC, LC-USZ62-70209.)

19

THOMAS RAOUL. Thomas visited Asheville first at age 10, returning in 1897 at age 20 to begin working on Albemarle Park. He was enthusiastic about coordinating with Gilbert and his father and sent regular letters on the progress to his mother in Atlanta. The roads and buildings (including their location, design, and construction), sewers, electricity, trees, and plants all fell partially under his purview. (JRBP, Emory.)

GEORGE E. WARING JR., ENGINEER. Waring was an early advocate and designer of systems to separate sewage and storm-water runoff. He engineered the draining and reconstruction of the lakes and ponds of Central Park. The civil engineering firm of Waring, Chapman & Farquhar of New York City and Newport supervised the installation of sewers and drains for Albemarle Park according to the designs of Waring. (Frederick Gutekunst.)

HELEN DOYLE RAOUL. Helen was the daughter of US Navy paymaster J.D. Doyle and Anna Bestor Doyle of Washington, DC. Anna Doyle and her two daughters, Helen and Kathleen, came to spend most of their time in Asheville rather than Washington. They rented Vanderbilt's villa, Sunnicrest, and were friends with the Connallys of neighboring Fernihurst. Helen's wedding to Thomas Raoul was in the front hall of The Manor in 1910. (JRBP, Emory.)

NORMAN AND LORING RAOUL, 1906. The brothers, Norman (left) and Loring (right), seen here by Galax Cottage, worked together to survey the park properties. Their brothers, Gaston and Thomas, studied engineering at Georgia Tech and also worked on projects, such as road construction. (RFP, Emory.)

THOMAS RAOUL ABOARD SS LOMBARDIA. Having left Albemarle Park to seek relief from his tuberculosis, Thomas Raoul (right) takes tea on deck with E.D. Nevin (left) in 1903. Subsequent travels took him to sanitariums in Wehrawald, Germany; Davos, Switzerland; and Oracle, Arizona. Although people came to Asheville's sanitariums with the same affliction, The Manor advertised that consumptives were not welcome to appease the healthy guests. (RFP, Emory.)

CAPT. LORING RAOUL, AROUND 1918. Thomas's younger brother was employed by the Albemarle Park Company. Loring pruned trees for $1.75 a day in 1907, arriving in Asheville by walking from Chattanooga's National Guard Camp. On a separate occasion, he worked as a stenographer and clerk and lived in the Lodge. During World War I, he served as a field artillery officer in France. His marriage to Mary Harrison took place at Fernbank, the Atlanta home of her parents. (RFP, Emory.)

RAOULS WITH LORILLARDS. Thomas and Helen Raoul are shown walking with Helen's sister Kathleen Lorillard and her husband, Beeckman Lorillard, of the Lorillard Tobacco Company family. The Lorillards summered in Galax Cottage. Lorillard's uncle, Pierre Lorillard IV, developed Tuxedo Park in New York beginning in 1885, where fine Shingle-style cottages were also rented or sold to family and friends, as was done in Albemarle Park. (JRBP, Emory.)

COSTUME PARTY AT ZEALANDIA. Friends Helen Raoul, Dr. Pinkney Herbert (Possum Trot Cottage), a Mrs. Henry, Mabel Morgan, Thomas Raoul, a Mrs. Mumminger, Vance Brown, a Mrs. Lewisohn, Jane Addams, Edith Vanderbilt (Biltmore House), and Philip Henry partied in the Henrys' home, Zealandia, designed by Richard Sharp Smith. Henry was a diplomat, scholar, and businessman who founded Asheville's first art museum at Zealandia. Thomas Wolfe wrote in Look Homeward, Angel about the estate and "Philip Roseberry," the pseudonym for Philip Henry. (JRBP, Emory.)

ELEONORE RAOUL. The youngest daughter of Mary and William Raoul, Eleonore worked with her mother in the movement for women's rights, cofounding the Fulton and DeKalb Equal Suffrage Party. A significant event occurred in 1915 during Atlanta's Harvest Festival celebration. Forced by the city to march last, behind city dump cars, hundreds of "radical" marchers wearing sashes and carrying banners were led by a brass band. Riding a white horse and representing the herald leading women "forward into light" was Eleonore Raoul. She would become the first woman to graduate from Emory University's School of Law. At the age of 85, Eleonore once again paraded down Peachtree Street, this time for ratification of the Equal Rights Amendment. (Both, RFP, Emory.)

RAOUL BROTHERS. The five brothers are shown in totem pole fashion against the front porch of Milfoil Cottage; from bottom to top are William Jr., Loring, Norman, Thomas, and Gaston. The three younger brothers worked with Thomas during the early development phase of the park by helping with surveying and roadwork. Their educational backgrounds in engineering and knowledge of railroad construction proved useful. (RFP, Emory.)

MADELON "GLORY" BATTLE HANCOCK. Helen Doyle (sixth from right), later Mrs. Thomas Raoul, attends to Madelon "Glory" Battle upon her wedding to British captain Mortimer Hancock. Madelon's father, Dr. Samuel Westray Battle (far right), was responsible for initiating Asheville's development as a health destination and also instituted its streetcar system. Glory would become the most decorated nurse for the Allied forces in World War I, receiving 12 decorations from Great Britain, Belgium, and France. (JRBP, Emory.)

RAOUL BROTHERS AND SISTERS. Since 1887, the entire Raoul family had spent occasional summers in Asheville. Most had participated in some development of the park and held fond memories of it. Here, eight siblings are gathered once again in front of Milfoil Cottage; they are, from left to right, (first row) Norman and Thomas; (second row) Rebecca, Mary, William, and Eleonore; (third row) Gaston and Loring. (RFP, Emory.)

THOMAS RAOUL WITH DOG. Thomas and his father, William Greene Raoul, took great satisfaction in building. Thomas's grandfather William Wadley was described similarly: "He seems to have been a man who always thought in terms of permanence. Wherever he stopped in his wanderings, he never 'squatted,' but always was founding an estate." (RFP, Emory.)

Three

FASHIONING A
CULTURAL LANDSCAPE

Although the concept of a cultural landscape can be traced to the European tradition of landscape painting, it was first used as an academic term by the German geographer Otto Schlüter in 1908 and further promoted in the 1920s by geographer Carl O. Sauer, a professor at the University of California at Berkeley who defined the cultural landscape as something "fashioned from a natural landscape by a culture group. Culture is the agent, the natural area is the medium, the cultural landscape is the result."

Albemarle Park, a resort community located on a former streetcar line in suburban Asheville and planned in the picturesque style, is one such cultural landscape. The picturesque style was influenced by the work of Andrew Jackson Downing and popularized by Frederick Law Olmsted, Calvert Vaux, and others in the late 19th century. The landscape design of the development was the vision of Samuel Parsons Jr., landscape architect for the City of New York, who had previously worked for Calvert Vaux's firm. Parsons appreciated the potential of the site despite its difficulties, and through a comprehensive study, including the use of a wax model, he overcame the challenges imposed by the steep terrain.

Charles Birnbaum, founder and president of the Cultural Landscape Foundation, who studied Parsons's work, writes, "Parsons found the site to a be a challenge, offering him opportunity to incorporate its rugged terrain, sweeping vistas, native stands of trees, and woodland vegetation as character defining features. Conceived in the picturesque style, the plan reinforced the unique natural and dramatic qualities of the landscape to establish a residential park that Parsons referred to as a 'homestead park.' "

In her memoir, *The Family of Raoul*, Mary Raoul Millis writes, "They selected a site on the slopes of the hills above Charlotte Street, facing west, whence the gorgeous sunsets of Carolina could be admired in all their glory."

THE NATURAL SETTING. In his book *How to Plan the Home Grounds*, published in 1901, Samuel Parsons describes the natural environment of Albemarle Park: "The whole region is a mountain hillside, with trees, shrubs and vines largely clothing its slopes and therefore the intention is evident everywhere of supplementing the work of Nature in the same spirit but with a distinct view of making tasteful and comfortable human homes within its confines." (RFP, Emory.)

ORIGINAL SCHEMATIC DESIGN WITH LONGITUDINAL CROSS SECTION. With an average slope of 20 percent, further complicated by a ridge running through the center with depressions on either side, Parsons believed the site unsuitable for residential development. But appreciating the beautiful mountain view, he designed each lot to its full advantage. The road system is well integrated, with buffer plantings and hillside steps connecting cottages to the road. (Samuel Parsons.)

28

A RESIDENTIAL PARK. Samuel Parsons and his partner, George Pentecost, began laying out Albemarle Park in the late 1890s. As a leader in the emerging field of landscape architecture, Parsons chaired the subcommittee that developed the American Society of Landscape Architecture (ASLA) constitution adopted in 1899, concurrent with his work at Albemarle Park. He was excited about the opportunity to work with Gilbert on the project, despite the difficulties and challenges imposed by the topography. His vision for Albemarle Park was to reinforce the unique, inherent natural and dramatic qualities of the landscape, acknowledging the *genius loci*, or spirit of the place. The creation of a residential or homestead park through the thoughtful and comprehensive arrangement of drives, walks, residences, and plant material for the aesthetic enjoyment and comfort of the guests was groundbreaking for its time. (Both, NCC, Pack.)

ALBEMARLE PARK OVERVIEW. Looking northwest toward Reynolds Mountain, formerly Gooch Peak, Crow's Nest, Shamrock, and Milfoil Cottages are visible from left to right in the foreground. Clover and Cherokee Cottages sit in front of The Manor, then Clematis, Columbus, Clio, and Galax Cottages follow from left to right. The mountainous terrain and sweeping vistas offered by the site are apparent. (RFP, Emory.)

A MINIATURE PARK FOR CHEROKEE COTTAGE. Samuel Parsons was able to apply his experience from planning public parks, cemeteries, and estates across the country to meet his client's needs. Through shared vistas, he ensured that each lot in the development availed itself of the site's natural beauty, creating for each property its own "miniature park." (EMB, Ramsey.)

CHEROKEE ROAD. An adequate drainage system was first on the agenda when constructing the park, and the Raouls spared no expense in its construction. Designed by George E. Waring and Samuel Parsons with oversight by Thomas Raoul and his brothers, it could handle the worst "torrential rains." Brick swales are visible here on Cherokee Road, as are the trees used to "temper the rays of the sun." (NCC, Pack.)

THE ROAD DOWN TO THE CLUBHOUSE. The road system of Albemarle Park, viewed by Parsons as a necessary evil, was originally constructed with gravel over a macadam foundation and designed with a maximum grade of 14 percent, enabling a carriage to pass down "with some degree of comfort," according to Parsons. (RFP, Emory.)

BREEZEMONT WITH STONE WALL. Retaining walls along the roads were another feature that Parsons believed should be used sparingly out of necessity and never as a barrier. He approved of graceful rounded stone caps and the play of light and shade achieved through the use of rough native stone. Stone for construction of the walls was quarried by Thomas Raoul on the south side of the property. (RSSR.)

THE VEGETATED ROADWAYS. The roads and drives were planted in an irregular pattern among mixed vegetation consisting of native trees, such as American ash, tulip poplar, American linden, oak, maple, and cherrie, and mixed with shrubs like spiraea, forsythia, itea, and red twigged dogwood. Parsons's favorites were the vines and creepers he planted along the steep road banks, which he believed harmonized with the rugged terrain. (NCC, Pack.)

THE GREENSWARD BY THE CLUBHOUSE. "A little open meadow with moderately sloping hillsides is retained near the entrance, where only is to be noticed any considerable stretch of turf for greensward," stated Parsons. A flight of steps leads up to The Manor. This area was used as a children's playground, and The Manor management employed guardians to watch over the youngsters. Advertising brochures emphasized the benefits of having a special space allotted for children, considered "bugbears at most hotels and resorts," to play. (Above, RFP, Emory; below, NCC, Pack.)

THE CLUBHOUSE LAWN AND FURNISHINGS. The low profile of the Clubhouse, also known as the Casino, blends naturally into the lawn accentuated with trees. A small fountain and rustic benches were among the few ornamental features found on the site, as Parsons's vision did not include embellishments such as urns or statuary. (RSSR.)

A FOGGY AUTUMN MORNING. Manicured lawns are juxtaposed against the wildflower meadow with plantings of asters and daisies that will turn white in the spring. The preeminence of the landscape is expressed with cottage names such as Crow's Nest, Dahlia, Daffodil, Hollyhock, Marigold, and Orchard, all pictured here. (RFP, Emory.)

KALMIA AND MILFOIL. Parsons worked closely with Gilbert, carefully studying the layout of each lot, which ranged in size from one-half to three acres. The mid and upper slopes of the property had not been cleared for farming, leaving the native forests of chestnut and oak. The layout of the cottages retained these natural forested areas whenever possible. (State Archives.)

ALBEMARLE PARK ENTRANCE LOOKING UP CHEROKEE ROAD. The Lodge served as the picturesque lower entrance to Albemarle Park and was lavishly landscaped with honeysuckle, English ivy, and rose. (RSSR.)

35

RUNNING PRAIRIE ROSE. *Rosa setigera*, a species native to America, adorns the Lodge. This species was widely used by Parsons and to him was the "crowning improvement" of his roadside "plantations," as it harmonized well with the natural landscape. He also considered it the best vine suited to the steep hillsides because of its vigorous growth, healthy foliage, and profusion of blooms. (RFP, Emory.)

CLEMATIS COTTAGE, AROUND 1903. Hydrangeas are massed along the circular driveway, accentuated with larger shrubs, while vines trail along the stone foundation. Parsons ordered most of the plant material for Albemarle Park from Chauncey Beadle at the Biltmore Nursery, which was created to grow material for landscaping the grounds of the Biltmore Estate. (RFP, Emory.)

COLUMBUS COTTAGE. Built in 1898, Columbus was the first cottage completed. The area north of the cottage, outside of Albemarle Park, was still in farm use. Fencing was used on a limited basis and primarily found around the perimeter of the development. Locust bollards with two horizontal wires were used in some of the common areas. Though delineating a private space, the fencing is nearly invisible and would eventually be covered in vegetation. The view below, also of Columbus, depicts a more mature landscape and the absence of the original fence. (Above, State Archives; below, FK.)

MATURATION OF THE LANDSCAPE AT THE MANOR. Parsons had a solid understanding of individual plant needs and growth characteristics, expertly arranging horticultural material to achieve a natural effect that would remain vigorous for many years, requiring little in the form of cultivation, pruning, or other maintenance. Parsons wrote, "These landscape features should be managed so as to make us think of the most charming effects of woodland and meadow, though not to deceive, but instead, exclaim how well the grouping is contrived for the open meadows and lawns and long vistas of the place, and at the same time for the individual exhibition of the native charms of the trees and shrubs." (Above, RSSR; below, EMB, Ramsey.)

FOOTBRIDGE TO BROWN BEAR. This rustic-style footbridge spanned a distance of 125 feet across a ravine, connecting the twin cottages of Wildfell and Brown Bear to Cherokee Road. By 1960, it had fallen into disrepair and was removed. Parsons believed that rustic architectural features such as bridges or fences should never be introduced unless their practical advantage was paramount. The bridge had been used as access to Brown Bear Cottage for the delivery of coal, its primary heating source. Once the bridge was removed, the house was refitted to use a natural gas heating system. (Alan Shaw.)

THE RUSTIC LAMPPOST. These lighting fixtures were part of the original design. The luminaries were similar to the those used in Biltmore Village but were mounted to locust posts, which were naturally rot resistant and better suited to the rustic architecture and naturalistic landscape style of Albemarle Park. (RFP, Emory.)

A PROFUSION OF DOGWOODS. Loring Raoul wrote to his mother in April 1909: "The spring growth is just at its best now. The dogwood has come around and the sides of the mountains show every imaginable shade of green." Not being a horticulturist, Loring had a difficult time answering endless questions from The Manor's guests concerning plant names. (NCC, Pack.)

WISTERIA ON THE MANOR. While beautiful draped over a side porch of The Manor, *Wisteria sinenses*, the Chinese species, has proven to be extremely invasive; the less invasive American species, *frutescens*, is now preferred for use in the region. William Greene and Mary Raoul were also plant enthusiasts and delighted in adding their own personal touches to the landscape. (RSSR.)

A SENSIBLE BEAUTY. To Parsons, the practical as well as the aesthetic needs of a site were important for the success of the project. His vision espoused a sensibility of design that included a relationship between all the individual parts of the landscape, giving it a dignified and sensible beauty that would charm the visitor and was meant to last. (NCC, Pack.)

Four

A MOUNTAIN
RESORT ARCHITECTURE

The late 19th century brought prosperity to America and with that an unprecedented number of tourists journeying to new locations. Architects looked nostalgically to colonial America architecture for inspiration to create an original American resort style—the Shingle style. Bradford Gilbert based his Albemarle Park designs in this style. Shingle-style houses were "the freest and on the whole, among the most generous forms that the United States has yet produced . . . in their own way they were also the gentlest forms: the most relaxed and spiritually open and . . . the most wholly wedded to the landscape," wrote Vincent Scully. This style was combined with English Tudor and Queen Anne for the early core buildings of the park. Appalachian rustic, Craftsman, and other styles were added in following years, and the site allowed for harmony between the buildings. Access to the outdoors via porches, balconies, terraces, and repeated windows supported the popular "fresh air" way of life. This fenestration broke any plane into another asymmetrical collage of light and shadow composed of the many textured surfaces. Pebbledash stucco, large timbers, wooden shingles, and stone foundations buttressed by large stone and brick chimneys provided a rich, indigenous palette of materials. However, the persistent links between buildings' interiors and the outdoors kept them light, friendly, and comfortable.

GATE LODGE. The Lodge was built just outside the city limits on Charlotte Street. Thomas Raoul wrote, "One winter a prospective boarder approached and I could hear his hack horses churning through the mud. He at last reached the port of safety and came in with the declaration that he would be damned if he would stay in such a hotel if it were not for the fact that it was so hard to get away." (NCC, Pack.)

THE MANOR AND LODGE, AROUND 1898. This early photograph was taken before the 1903 wing addition and prior to landscaping. The Manor stands three and a half stories with asymmetrical shingled gables over timbers and heavy stucco on a stone foundation. The left gable has a saltbox form, the center is higher with flared eaves, and the right gable is gambrel. The original inn was built for $20,000, enough to cause a sensation at the time. (NCC, Pack.)

GATE LODGE, 1930S. The Lodge, with its cone-roofed tower and open arches, was a prelude to the greater inn. The ground floor is composed of stone, timbers, and stucco; the second floor is shingled with a flared skirt. Hammered metal letters on the arch spelled "Albemarle Park" when The Manor Gate Bookhouse Rental Library occupied part of the Lodge. (NCC, Pack.)

THE MANOR FROM SOUTH. This view shows the 1903 wing on the left with its massive chimney and half-timbering. The two-story canted oriel window hangs above the arched ground floor ballroom windows. The large ballroom windows pivot in from the top to allow airflow or cleaning. (RFP, Emory.)

THE MANOR FROM CLUBHOUSE LAWN. The Manor was intended to give the impression of a rambling country house. The curved porches to the right provided an overlook of the lawn and tennis courts at the Clubhouse, across Cherokee Road. Bradford Gilbert named The Manor, perhaps inspired by the family's French name, Raoul de Champmanoir, or Ralph of the Field Manor. (RFP, Emory.)

THE MANOR FROM CHARLOTTE STREET. Thomas Raoul hired prominent builder and architect James Tennent to construct The Manor and several cottages. Raoul wrote that the standard price of construction labor was 75¢ per day; carpenters got $1.50 and masons a little more. The Manor opened for business on New Year's Eve 1898. (RSSR.)

STROLLING ON THE MANOR LAWN. A walk about the grounds becomes an opportunity for a photograph with The Manor as backdrop. The use of textured building materials and hand craftsmanship gave an aged character to Albemarle Park's appearance early on. Timbers reveal marks of hand tools, and the chimney's stone base transitions to brick. (HCJBRP, Ramsey.)

EAST FACADE OF THE MANOR. The porte cochere over the driveway marks the main entrance to The Manor. Wooden shingles wrap the roof, gables, and the walls of the upper level. Seven chimneys seem to stake the building to the earth. This photograph was taken before the 1914 wing was added to the right, which eliminated the rooftop porch. (RFP, Emory.)

PORTE COCHERE OF THE MANOR, AROUND 1951. A valet stands at the former carriage entrance to the main building. Here, the wooden roof shakes have been replaced with French diagonal pattern shingles. This was the last decade of The Manor's operation as a hotel. (NCC, Pack.)

SUSIE IN THE MANOR HALL. The entrance hall adjoining the porte cochere is warmed by a large brick fireplace. Susie Saxon, who worked as a domestic, waitress, and seneschal at The Manor for over 19 years, used bells and chimes to signal guests for meals. In 1928, an open letter of thanks to Thomas Raoul from Albemarle Park employees was published in the newspaper and was signed by Susie. (NCC, Pack.)

PEACOCK ALLEY. The window-lined corridor was dubbed Peacock Alley from earlier decades when the daily promenade of ladies wearing fashionably plumed hats and gowns provided spectacle. In response to the larger issue of some bird species facing extinction due to plume hunting, Theodore Roosevelt established the first American wildlife refuge in Florida in 1903, a year after visiting Asheville. (JRBP, Emory.)

THE MANOR HALL FIREPLACE. This photograph, taken in the mid-20th century, shows surfaces repainted and new wallpaper replacing the original red burlap described by Thomas Raoul in a letter. The double-sided fireplace retained its large andirons and Susie's chimes. The writing room is seen through the doorways. (NCC, Pack.)

THE MANOR SITTING ROOM. Several public rooms gave guests options for various activities. "Every effort is made to have the place as nearly like a home as a public house can well be made, and in carrying out this idea, all the conventional hotel features which are not essential to a proper service are eliminated," described a promotional booklet. (FK.)

THE SITTING ROOM. This photograph, taken a few decades after the previous image, shows brighter paint colors, new lighting, and draperies, with wicker and oriental rugs as seen earlier. A man reads the newspaper by a piano in front of the fireplace. (NCC, Pack.)

APPROACHING CLOVER COTTAGE. The drive on Cherokee and Terrace Roads rounds the tower of Clover Cottage. Textured forms and materials merge with living plants, forming a bounteous architectural collage. "Thirty-three yards from the Manor, lighted by electricity; heated by hot air and hot water; six bed-rooms; two sitting rooms with open fire-place; one bath-room with hot and cold water; two porches; telephone. Be relieved of the cares of housekeeping, as this is attended to by the hotel servants, the occupants taking their meals at The Manor," advertised an early brochure. (RFP, Emory.)

CLOVER COTTAGE, AROUND 1898. The architecture of The Manor is scaled down to cottage size here; similar forms and materials are repeated but on a more intimate scale. Wooden shakes cover the roof, gables, and upper walls, supported by a timber-and-stucco main floor on a coursed rubble stone foundation. The former farm landscape remained in the background. (State Archives.)

CLOVER COTTAGE AT CHEROKEE ROAD. Clover Cottage's tower is mounted with a circular porch overlooking the greensward and Clubhouse, where sporting events took place. Engineer George E. Waring's brick storm-water gutter was traversed by a stone slab step. (RFP, Emory.)

COLUMBUS COTTAGE. Architectural features seen on other Albemarle Park buildings, including informal asymmetrical massing, hooded windows, and timbers on a stone foundation, were reconfigured to form this charming cottage. The gable (left) is patterned with a wave of shingles that transition down the eaves, brackets, hooded window, and wall to the flared skirt. (RFP, Emory.)

CLEMATIS COTTAGE. Known as Laurel Cottage today, its prominent feature is the bay window where roofs converge above the granite steps to the porch. Interesting details are the shingled brackets and the eyebrow window. Clematis was "let in suites of two, three of our rooms with private bath" with a total of nine bedrooms, describes an advertising booklet. People on the vine-framed porch show the scale. (NCC, Pack.)

FOXHALL, CLEMATIS, AND CHEROKEE COTTAGES. The location and orientation of the cottages allows for privacy as well as connectivity, all in harmony with the contours of the mountainside. In this photograph from around 1914, Foxhall shares similar features with Gilbert's cottage designs even though it was designed by Neel Reid. (NCC, Pack.)

CLIO COTTAGE. This shingled adaptation of a Swiss chalet has an intriguing facade with large, two-tiered brackets and a patterned wooden pediment screen. Shed dormers penetrate the roof, and Union Jack–patterned balustrades salute "an English Inn in America." Clio is the muse of history from Greek mythology. (State Archives.)

GALAX COTTAGE. The Dutch Colonial Revival style is adapted for this mountainside resort location. Natural wooden shingles covered the walls and intersecting gambrel roofs. Diamond-patterned upper sash windows could be shuttered. The deep porch, with both shaded and sunny areas, overlooked Circle Park. It was advertised as "Four bed-rooms and bath on second floor; large sitting room, study, dining room, kitchen and pantry on ground floor; two servants' rooms, servants' bath-room, laundry, furnace and fuel room in basement." Albemarle Park's stables were located behind Galax, and the macadam roads were well suited for equestrian use. (Both, State Archives.)

MANZANITA COTTAGE. Thomas Raoul selected this site, apart from The Manor and amidst trees, for his own home and retreat. Impressive rough granite chimneys punctuate wooden shingled walls. Tree trunk columns support the graceful hip roof above the deep porch. A bedroom wing was added when Thomas married Helen. (FK.)

POSSUM TROT COTTAGE. Dr. William Pinkney Herbert built his home in a Rustic Mountain style in 1914. Tree limbs and trunks were used structurally indoors and out. Herbert was writer O. Henry's doctor and loaned his medical books to him as reference material. Herbert was a friend of the Raouls and would eventually relocate with them to the new Biltmore Forest. Construction pioneer Luther L. Merchant was the contractor. (APMGA.)

MILFOIL COTTAGE. Characteristic of Bradford Gilbert's designs, Milfoil has the large timbered framing and shingled exterior. Built as a housekeeping cottage, it became a favorite of Thomas Raoul, who moved there as his family grew. In 1920, his other Albemarle Park properties were sold to E.W. Grove, but Thomas retained Milfoil and Dogwood. (APMG.)

JANE RAOUL IN MILFOIL, 1918. Three-year-old Jane Raoul (later Bingham) sits in her family's home. Deep bay windows, textured plaster, and oak trim distinguish the interior. Milfoil's cove ceilinged living room was re-created at Raoulwood in Biltmore Forest in 1922. (RFP, Emory.)

ORCHARD COTTAGE. Shamrock and Orchard Cottages share a somewhat different appearance from Gilbert's designs. They were slightly more formal, and each had a reception hall. Atlanta's W.T. Downing was a contributing Albemarle Park architect and possibly the designer. More traditional forms and vertical emphases distinguish them. Orchard had "a large porch, partially enclosed with removable sash," describes an advertising booklet. (Charles and Cherry Livengood.)

SHAMROCK COTTAGE. Built in 1898 as a housekeeping cottage, Shamrock had eight rooms plus a bath on the upper floors with servants' room and utilities in the basement. Newlyweds Dr. Thomas Patton Cheesborough and Alice Kerr Connally, of Fernihurst, took residence in Shamrock in 1900. A tuberculosis specialist practicing with Dr. Battle, Cheesborough married in All Souls Episcopal Church in 1900. Seven years later, he rented the historic Smith-McDowell house, as would Herbert Miles during the construction of Breezemont. (Robert Sauer.)

Ramsey Family at Orchard Cottage, around 1924. Lucy and Simeon Clay Ramsey owned Orchard Cottage after being neighbors of Thomas Wolfe on Woodfin Street. Their only son, D. Hiden Ramsey, became associate editor of the *Citizen*, editor of the *Asheville Times*, and general manager of the *Citizen-Times* Company for over 30 years. He was also a public speaker, city and state official, writer, education advocate, and sportsman. D. Hiden Ramsey Library at the University of North Carolina bears his name. (NCC, Pack.)

DOGWOOD COTTAGE. William Greene Raoul built his home about 1907 above Circle Park with a western view. The Rustic style was fully employed by use of large foundation stones, tree trunk columns, and branch railings. The exterior walls, and presumably the original roof, used wooden shingles from chestnut trees, now nearly extinct. The main interior rooms were often one room deep, allowing for maximum ventilation, natural light, and a sense of place. (RFP, Emory.)

WILLIAM GREENE RAOUL AT DOGWOOD. Looking out from his western porch is Captain Raoul. Thomas Raoul wrote, "Father had about as much pleasure from his building in Asheville as he did from anything in his life . . . every time he built a new cottage he felt like a little boy who buys a new toy—that he really should not put so much money into the venture, but it was so much fun!" (RFP, Emory.)

VIEW FROM CHEROKEE COTTAGE, 1921. The silhouette of the timbered porch frames a view of the Lodge entrance (left), Clover Cottage, The Manor, and Clematis (right edge). The chimney of the boiler house can be seen in the center behind The Manor; the Grove Park neighborhood is developing in the distance. (EMB, Ramsey.)

CHEROKEE COTTAGE. The refined, lodge-like architecture of Cherokee Cottage celebrates its location on Sunset Mountain. Porches open to the outdoors from three levels, with stairs leading down to the earth below, and shingle patterns change. Originally, it contained 14 bedrooms and 4 baths that were lit by electricity. (RSSR.)

WILDFELL AND BROWN BEAR COTTAGES. With mountainside rusticity, these cottages were sited above a creek bed and were originally accessed by a wooden foot bridge. Porches structured with logs and branches and multilevel interiors conjure an unconventional tree house or bunkhouse character. The cottages border a 150-foot-long stone retaining wall, originally constructed by the Raouls and later rebuilt. (APMGA.)

ORCHARD ROAD PASSING CLUBHOUSE. The macadam road curves around the sloping mountain contours above the drum-like room of the Clubhouse, which contained a circular bench for the bowling alley. The stone gutters are bridged with stone slabs. (RSSR)

ROSEBANK COTTAGE. Rosebank displays the Dutch Colonial and Shingle styles used in American resorts. A lively fenestration of clustered and bay windows, overhangs, hoods, and chunky rafter tails sit atop the rustic stone foundation. Prominent senator Luke Lea, founder of the *Tennessean* newspaper, lived several seasons here during the 1910s. Lea endured a controversial trial and imprisonment as a result of the failure of Asheville's Central Bank and Trust Company, though he claimed accusations were politically motivated. (RFP, Emory.)

ALVA GLEN. This half-timbered, Arts and Crafts–style cottage was built for railroad president James W. Archibald in 1913. Archibald named it after a spectacular gorge in his native Scotland. Lyman Beecher, grandson of social reformer Henry Ward Beecher, brother to Harriet Beecher Stowe, bought Alva Glen from Archibald. Lyman's daughter, Mary Beecher, married William F.P. Coxe in 1926. William was the grandson of Col. Frank Coxe and son of Tench Coxe. (RSSR.)

LARKSPUR COTTAGE. Larkspur was an existing house that was relocated to Border Row. An alleyway south of the house leads to the location of the former Albemarle Park public garage on Charlotte Street. Edward S. Massey managed the garage, provided "auto livery," and lived in Larkspur around 1918. (RFP, Emory.)

64

BORDER ROW COTTAGES. Cottages along a southern boundary of Albemarle Park were called the Border Row Cottages. They are sited in a linear manner and have access to Charlotte Street via Hillside Walk, a brick sidewalk. Hollyhock, Marigold, and Larkspur Cottages are shown in this early photograph. Note the curved second-floor window jambs that give greater depth and interest to the walls. (RFP, Emory.)

MARIGOLD COTTAGE. Marigold and Hollyhock are from a Bradford Gilbert design for a dependency built at William Greene Raoul's Peachtree Street estate in Atlanta. The Raouls favored the design well enough to replicate it in Albemarle Park, twice. The arches, overhanging gable, exposed rafter ends, and shingled upper levels are features seen in Gilbert's portfolio. (RFP, Emory.)

DAFFODIL COTTAGE. Craftsman-style bungalow characteristics are seen in Daffodil Cottage, such as a front porch, plain balustrade, story and a half with dormers, natural materials, and structure in place of ornamentation. A hybrid roof of hip and gable forms is employed. The unusually deep eaves with exposed rafters are a strong design element. (RFP, Emory.)

DAHLIA COTTAGE. Dahlia and Daffodil are twins with mirrored plans and once shared the same entrance pathway. Brick was used for the foundations and chimneys, with wooden shingled roofs and walls. These cottages were close enough to Dr. Von Ruck's grand house to hear the Aeolian pipe organ from his two-story music room. (RFP, Emory.)

CROW'S NEST COTTAGE. This rustic cottage was perched over the greensward below. The stone entrance leads into a two-story room with a fireplace and arched window. Tree trunks and limbs were used for structuring, and stone and wooden shingles created an enchanting home that is one with its natural surroundings. (RFP, Emory.)

CROW'S NEST STUDIO. Early references to "Crow's Nest Studio" suggest that the cottage might have been conceived as a separate location to explore artistic endeavors. Tuberculosis specialist Dr. Frazer Thompson lived here in 1909. Thompson served on the board of the Asheville Horse Show with Thomas Raoul and worked at Biltmore Hospital. Loring attended a bridge party the Thompsons gave but wrote, "I managed not to get there until the chafing dish supper started." (EMB, Ramsey.)

SNUG HARBOR. Three cottages are accessed prior to Albemarle Park's Lodge entrance from Charlotte Street. Snug Harbor is a Tudor-like, Arts and Crafts–style cottage on a slope with a long western view. (APMGA.)

LOCUST COTTAGE. Locust and Fir Tree Cottages sit side by side on Charlotte Street and exemplify Arts and Crafts–style bungalows from the original period of the revived style. Divided upper sash windows, bracketed soffits, entrances through porches, plain balustrades, and shingled walls are found in both cottages. (APMGA.)

Five

BUILDING ON
THE FOUNDATION

Albemarle Park's original architect, Bradford Gilbert, died in 1911; William Greene Raoul died shortly after in 1913. The original idea of selling lots had been put aside since William Greene took such great pleasure in building cottages, and none of the property was sold during his lifetime. The strength of the architecture influenced succeeding builders. Herbert D. Miles selected the English-born Richard Sharp Smith to design his home, Breezemont. Smith's design was more formal but continued English themes. When Edwin Wiley Grove purchased The Manor and additional properties from Thomas Raoul in 1920, he also chose Smith and his partner, Albert Heath Carrier, for three new building plans. A young Atlanta architect named J. Neel Reid designed two cottages, Kalmia and Foxhall. Reid would become the best-known residential architect in Atlanta, working later in Colonial and Classical styles. The Georgia Trust awards the J. Neel Reid Prize yearly to an architecture student, intern, or recently registered architect for study travel that honors the legacy of Neel Reid. Another local architect had a smaller role; William Waldo Dodge was hired to design additions to The Manor and the Clubhouse. Dodge was a craftsman who hand-wrought silver, carved wood, and designed buildings in the Tudoresque style. The modern sensibility of the 1950s–1960s would bring a few buildings that might now seem out of place, but most new construction has been appropriate to the original spirit.

RICHARD SHARP SMITH. Born in Yorkshire in 1852, Smith immigrated to the United States from England in 1882 and worked for Bradford Gilbert in New York, supervising construction of railroad stations before joining the offices of Richard Morris Hunt in 1886. He arrived in Asheville as resident and supervising architect for the Biltmore Estate in 1889. Smith is seated on the right; his longtime partner, Heath Carrier, stands next to him. (NCC, Pack.)

OFFICE OF SMITH AND CARRIER. Richard Sharp Smith established his own practice in Asheville in 1895 and in 1906 formed a partnership with Albert Heath Carrier that lasted until his death in 1924. This was their office, located on Church Street from 1906 to 1910. Charles Parker, architect of Raoulwood, worked with the firm from 1909 to 1913, prior to their Albemarle Park commissions. (NCC, Pack.)

CHUNNS COVE, RESIDENCE OF RICHARD SHARP SMITH, AROUND 1906. Smith became the region's most prolific architect. Trained by his cousin in Manchester, he introduced an English tradition of architecture to the area, creatively combining local materials, as exemplified here at Stoneybrook. He left an indelible influence on the architecture of Asheville, designing numerous homes in Montford, Chestnut Hill, and Grove Park. He also designed significant public buildings around the region. (NCC, Pack.)

YOUNG MEN'S INSTITUTE, AROUND 1905. Commissioned by George Vanderbilt and designed by R.S. Smith in 1892, this structure was used to house an institution to improve the moral fiber of the black men who worked on the Biltmore Estate through education focused on social, cultural, business, and religious life. Pictured here are Maggie Jones, Edward Pearson, James Vester Miller, Dr. Lee Miller, and others who worked to purchase the Tudor-style building from Vanderbilt. (NCC, Pack.)

Breezemont under Construction, 1914. Smith drew from his English architectural vocabulary for the style, massing, and materials used for Breezemont. The character of a smaller English country house derives from Tudor, Palladian, and Georgian features. Open air is accessed via porches, balconies, and a terrace. The initial Breezemont design envisioned a larger footprint for the house. (RSSR.)

Breezemont Christmas Card, 1916. The Miles family sent a photographic Christmas card of their two-year-old home. The terrace stairs are countered by a sloping roofline that divides a Tudoresque section containing the sleeping porch. Large windows face the western mountains. Dentil moulding and balusters create patterns of light and shadow. (RSSR.)

THE MILES FAMILY AT BREEZEMONT. Herbert Miles sits with daughters Eleanor and Marjorie and wife Delia Gallup Miles in their living room. An inglenook is formed by the arched brick fireplace flanked by built-in benches. Bookcases, window seats, and oak trim are in the Arts and Crafts style. French doors and sidelights allow for light and air to pass through the main floor. (RSSR.)

TWIN OAKS. Architects Smith and Carrier designed this apartment house with Tudor Revival details for Edwin Wiley Grove in 1920. Its architecture is similar to Chipmunk and Chestnut Hill Cottages, also by these architects, and its porches are present on three floors. (NCC, Pack.)

CHIPMUNK COTTAGE. Chipmunk sat on a lushly landscaped site above the Circle Park, surrounded with trees. Architects Smith and Carrier planned the stone foundation, brick quoining, stucco, and half-timbering topped with an intersecting gambrel roof. The open porch had a stuccoed balustrade with timber framing. The Manor's own boiler house piped steam to the radiators of these cottages. E.W. Grove requested that the architects investigate hollow tile brick construction for the new buildings in 1920. (Above, NCC, Pack; below, RSSR.)

CARRIER'S QUADRANT CASEMENT ADJUSTER. Albert Heath Carrier, of Smith and Carrier Architects, used his own patented window hardware design for Chipmunk Cottage. The Adjuster was a lever-operated mechanism that pivoted a casement window a few inches from its edge, giving access to both sides from the interior. It can be pulled open from the outside and "does not interfere with screens or draperies," according to the advertisement at right. (RSSR.)

DODGE ADDITION TO THE MANOR WITH POOL, 1950. William Waldo Dodge Jr., a founding member of the Asheville architectural firm Six Associates, was a master craftsmen and architect. Originally from Washington, DC, he came to Asheville following a World War I exposure to chlorine gas that aggravated his tuberculosis. He studied to be a silver and copper smith while convalescing at the Veteran's Hospital in Oteen, later opening a shop and office in Biltmore Forest. (NCC, Pack.)

KALMIA COTTAGE. Loring and Thomas Raoul named Kalmia and started sketching elevation ideas for their father to review in 1910. Architect Neel Reid, however, drew the actual plans for the housekeeping cottage that year. Reid continued the use of natural construction materials, which were profusely festooned with vines, blending architecture into the landscape. (FK.)

FOXHALL (FOXHALL HILL). The second Neel Reid design for Albemarle Park was Foxhall and the renderings, dated 1912–1913, were prepared for the Albemarle Park Company. It was sold to Edgar A. and Ann Brook Fordtran, who had a home in Audubon Place, New Orleans's most elite enclave. (Robert Sauer.)

76

Six

THE GREAT OUTDOORS

The cultural changes brought about in the 19th century due to the industrial revolution also affected the popular attitude toward recreation and leisure activities in the United States. As more people left the rural areas to find work in cities, they were increasingly exiled from the natural environment. Technological advances in mechanization led to a reduction in work hours for the labor force, creating more time for leisure activities. Additionally, there was a growing belief that leisure could contribute to the idealistic liberal values that were part of the American intellectual heritage envisioned by Jefferson and Adams. Gradually, the social attitude toward leisure became more receptive, balancing the strong work ethic that had characterized the country during the colonial period when leisure activities were not looked upon in a favorable light. The latter part of the 19th century saw improvements in health care and life expectancy, the growth of public recreation in American cities, and the acceptance of the participation of women in outdoor and leisure activities. Travel to natural areas was also a growing trend, spurred by the 1869 publication of a wilderness guidebook to the Adirondacks by William H. Murray and the formation of the Sierra Club in 1892.

Nationally, tourism was burgeoning due to the growth of the railroad industry. Commercial amusement parks were often built on the outskirts of towns, and transit companies would offer reduced fare rides in decorated trolley cars. Overlook Park on the top of Sunset Mountain followed this trend, with a merry-go-round, concert pavilion, and open air trolley rides offering the finest panoramic views. Amusements and other outdoor activities were a large draw for visitors to Albemarle Park, and early brochures advertised the many activities available to guests.

OUTDOORS AT ALBEMARLE PARK. The Raouls appreciated the benefits of outdoor activities and designed the entire landscape of Albemarle Park with the benefits of health, recreation, and outdoor activities in mind. Footpaths wound their way around the cottages, and visitors could stroll down to the lawn below Crow's Nest to watch croquet tournaments and archery contests. (FK.)

THE ALBEMARLE CLUB. Thomas Raoul built a clubhouse on The Manor grounds in 1902, close to Charlotte Street near the Lodge. Early brochures advertised that pool and billiard tables, a bowling alley, and tennis courts were available for guests to enjoy. It essentially was an amusement park just outside The Manor door. (NCC, Pack.)

TENNIS AT ALBEMARLE PARK. Located adjacent to the Clubhouse, the tennis courts were the scene of many tournaments. Surrounding the courts were sloping, shady lawns furnished with rustic benches, offering spectators a pleasurable viewing experience, second only to the pleasure of playing. Clarence Hobart, six-time winner of the US National Tennis Championship, spent a season at Albemarle Park. Hobart later died in Asheville in 1930. (RFP, Emory.)

THE BILLIARD ROOM AT THE CASINO. The billiard room and lounge on the interior of the Clubhouse, or Casino, is pictured here. A glimpse of the bowling alley is visible through the open door in the background. Bowling tournaments were held regularly for both men and women. (NCC, Pack.)

LORING AND HIS HORSE, KEW, AT THE STABLES. The Raouls appreciated the benefits of outdoor recreation and sought to provide a host of outdoor activities and amusements for their guests. The stables, located on the north side of the property behind Clio Cottage, housed the family's personal horses as well as horses for guests to ride. Loring Raoul, one of Thomas's brothers, managed the inn for a year, beginning in January 1909, while Thomas was away in Europe for his health. Loring wrote to his mother often about his camping trips and adventures traveling throughout the Western North Carolina backcountry on his favorite horse, Kew. He also participated in tennis and bowling tournaments and was an avid hiker. (RFP, Emory.)

Loring and Kew. Loring participated in Atlanta horse shows and wrote to his mother of riding Kew every morning to get him in good condition and ready for competition. (RFP, Emory.)

Dog and Pony, around 1917. The Miles family's Chihuahua and horse stand at the Breezemont entrance from Cherokee Road. R.S. Smith continued the English style of Breezemont by designing ball finials on the gate piers. (RSSR.)

DRIVING THROUGH THE BILTMORE ESTATE.
Before the advent of the automobile,
Thomas Raoul enjoyed leisurely Sunday
afternoon carriage rides through the
Biltmore Estate while courting Helen
Doyle, his future wife. (NCC, Pack.)

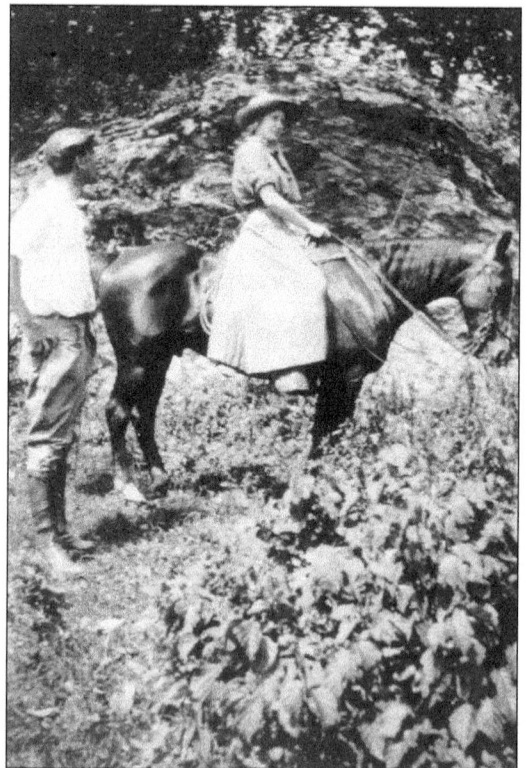

A RIDE ON CALAMITY, SUMMER 1909.
Helen Doyle is seen riding the Raouls'
horse Calamity, with Thomas Raoul
looking on. Helen and Thomas were
married in 1910. (RFP, Emory.)

GOLF AT THE ASHEVILLE COUNTRY CLUB. Located at the end of Charlotte Street a short distance from The Manor, the course was an amenity for guests to enjoy because of an arrangement Thomas Raoul had with the club, which allowed him to advertise the golf links. Concerned the club might lose the property, Thomas and his father considered purchasing it in 1905. (EMB, Ramsey.)

TENNIS AT THE ASHEVILLE COUNTRY CLUB. This shingled structure, designed by R.S. Smith and located on the 12th tee of the present-day Grove Park Inn course, replaced the original clubhouse, which was relocated to Edgemont Avenue in 1908. The clubhouse was short-lived, burning in down the early 1920s, and was replaced with the current Grove Park Inn Country Club Clubhouse in 1926. (NCC, Pack.)

ASHEVILLE COUNTRY CLUB PANORAMA, AROUND 1911. The club evolved out of the Swannanoa Country Club, originally organized in 1894, which was divided into the West Asheville Hunt Club, where fox hunting was the primary activity, and the downtown Town Club. With the growing interest in golf as a recreational activity, golf links (a reference to the original Scottish links-style courses characterized by the natural sandy, treeless, windswept environment of the Scottish coast) were established at various sites around Asheville, all of which proved unsatisfactory. In

1899, George W. Pack offered a five-year lease on some property at the end of Charlotte Street for a clubhouse, golf course, and other athletic sports. The name was changed in 1905 to the Country Club of Asheville. The first nine holes were designed by J.J. McCloskey, and by 1910, there were nine more holes designed by Willie Park. In 1913, the entire course was redesigned by Donald Ross. It is now part of the Grove Park Inn. (NCC, Pack.)

THE MANOR KITCHEN. Promotional brochures touted, "The table is good, supplied with the best fare, attractively served. Here the difference from the regular hotel is marked by the absence of the usual fancy French dishes, the table being very much like that of a well-conducted private house. The dining-room service is performed by quiet and efficient waitresses." (APMGA.)

THE DINING ROOM. This large room enabled the inn to serve up to 100 at one sitting. It was added in 1913 with the north wing expansion of The Manor. The dining experience in particular was used to distinguish the inn from the typical hotel or boardinghouse of its day. (NCC, Pack.)

AT THE FOOT OF THE CRAGGIES IN THE LAND OF THE SKY. In an early farm-to-table scenario, the Raouls sourced their food for The Manor from a local farm off Spooks Branch Road in the Beaverdam Valley. Thomas prodded his father to buy the farm and supervised its maintenance. He visited the farm, just a short horse ride of less than a mile over the ridge from Albemarle Park, every few days. (NCC, Pack.)

THE MILK SICK. Upon arriving in Albemarle Park, Loring wrote to the US Department of Agriculture concerning a mysterious cattle disease he had observed in the mountains called the "milk sick." Also called "trembles," it was thought to be a soil-borne disease. It was not until 1928 that the ingestion of white snakeroot was determined to be the cause. (NCC, Pack.)

RUSTIC ROADSIDE PAVILION. With the advent of the automobile for scenic touring, roadside architecture designed to lure people out of their cars became popular attractions across the countryside. The Sunset Mountain Autoway, following the route of the Sunset Park Railway, was built by E.W. Grove and stretched from the end of Charlotte Street to the summit of Sunset Mountain, nearly 1,000 feet above the city. (NCC, Pack.)

A WALK IN THE PARK, AROUND 1909. Dressed in Edwardian-era clothing, these visitors take in the view from Overlook Park, nearly 1,000 feet above the city. Loring Raoul wrote to his mother in the spring of 1909: "Sunset Mountain is my regular route when I go to walk with girls." (NCC, Pack.)

HIKING THE SUNSET TRAIL. This trail, also known as the Wander Trail, snaked its way up to Sunset Mountain from the Grove Park Inn. Rustic footbridges, steps, and signs marked the trail. E.W. Grove purchased the Overlook Park property, including the Sunset Park Railway, in 1911. (NCC, Pack.)

SURREY WITH THE FRINGE ON TOP. Binoculars in hand, these ladies take in the view from Sunset Mountain. The surrey, usually a two-seated pleasure carriage, takes its name from Surrey, England, where it was first made. (EMB, Ramsey.)

CRAGGY GARDENS. Upon a visit to Craggy in June 1909, Loring Raoul wrote, "The rhododendron was very pretty and in full bloom. I feel very much at home on Craggy now; I have been there so many times that I know all the trails and different views. Besides the rhododendron the fields were covered with daisies thicker than I have ever seen them, so that the fields looked white at a little distance." Craggy Gardens is a southern Appalachian heath bald, a mountaintop devoid of trees and vegetated with ericaceous shrubs, such as rhododendron, azalea, and mountain laurel. Their existence remains a mystery despite research into their origins. (EMB, Ramsey.)

Seven

MANNER OF LIVING

The Raoul family was educated, social, and enterprising. They wove into Albemarle Park's buildings and outdoor spaces opportunities for both relaxation and entertainment. One could find a quiet corner or outdoor bench for reading and writing, or a visit might include a concert or theater performance—indoors or alfresco. Creative and artistic personalities were attracted. Two Nobel Prize–winning writers stayed at The Manor: English novelist, playwright, and social activist John Galsworthy and Belgian playwright, poet, and essayist Maurice Maeterlinck. Asheville residents joined tourists in the ballroom, the scene of many events. A local teenager, Robert Bunn, attended dances between 1916 and 1918. One night, he grabbed a girl's arm to dance with her, and it was Cornelia Vanderbilt. They continued to dance many times for a few seasons. "She was an excellent dancer. She was tall, real light on her feet," Bunn recalled. Arthur Murray also attended and advised his students on their dance steps. Children were always around, in play yards and sometimes giving performances. On special days, friends would meet to watch the Asheville Horse Show in Riverside Park. And on occasion, a celebrity might visit and then report his or her experience. As residences became more permanent, quiet everyday lives took place in a charming setting.

HELEN AND THOMAS RAOUL
DINE ALFRESCO ON THE PORCH
OF MANZANITA COTTAGE. When
dining with others, as at The
Manor, "discussion of prices
while eating the meal outraged
one of the basic traditions of
southern gentility. A dictum,
not to be violated, was that
price of food should never be
alluded to except by those
providing it, and in the privacy
of the pantry," wrote Mary
Raoul Millis. (RFP, Emory.)

EAST TERRACE OF THE MANOR.
Comfortable rocking chairs
on the tiled terrace provided
a relaxed sitting area to
observe people arriving or
departing through the porte
cochere. The stone and brick
chimney, pebbledash stucco,
and wooden shingles provide
interesting natural textures, as
do the trees. Originally, a larger
terrace on the opposite side of
The Manor faced the western
mountains. (Albert Malone.)

THE MANOR BULLETIN,

From Albemarle Park, - - Asheville, N. C.

M _____

THE MANOR WRITING ROOM, ALBEMARLE PARK, ASHEVILLE, N. C.

THE MANOR BULLETIN. This folding postcard bulletin with a view of Cherokee Road and Cherokee Cottage and the writing room, where the fireplace opens to the entrance hall, was provided to guests. Postcards were a popular craze, comparable to today's social networking. A way to share travel experiences with friends and family, they were also advertisements. Landmarks, businesses, and curiosities were all of interest to a population traveling more for pleasure than any previously. (RSSR.)

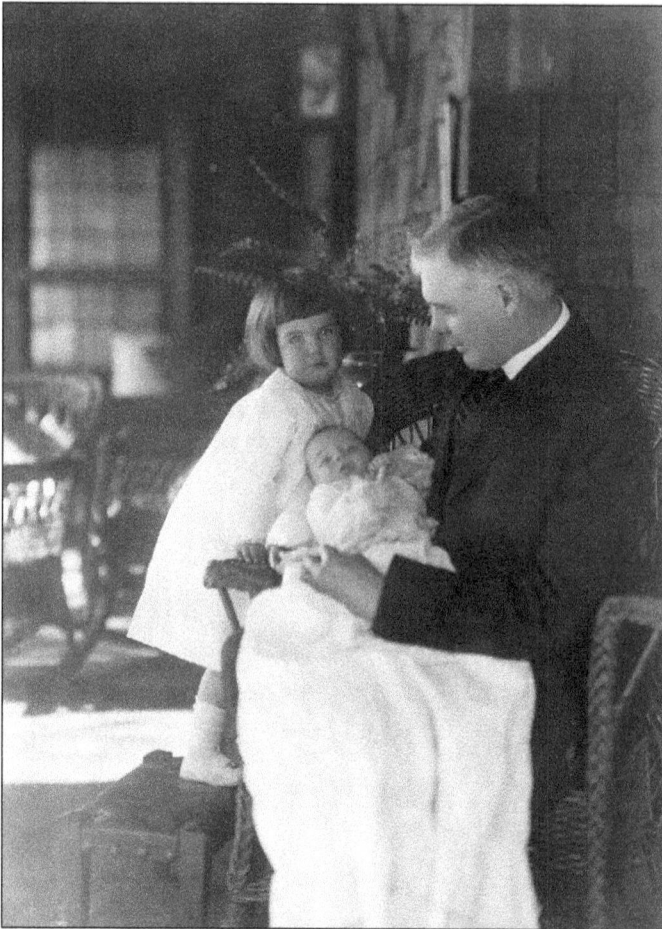

THOMAS WITH KATHLEEN AND JANE, AROUND 1915. Both daughters of Thomas and Helen Raoul were born in Manzanita Cottage. Porches found at Manzanita and throughout the park were used for tuberculosis relief. The girls attended L'Aria Fresca, at 236 Charlotte Street, an "out-of-door school for children of all ages" with classes "held throughout the year in the open air." (RFP, Emory.)

WALKWAY TO MANZANITA COTTAGE. Helen Raoul walks with her daughter as the nanny stands nearby. The 1910 addition to Manzanita, with its deep eaves, is seen in the background. (JRBP, Emory.)

CARRIAGE DRIVING ON CHARLOTTE STREET. Thomas and Helen Raoul are driven by Brooks just outside of Albemarle Park, on the road that Thomas had upgraded. Driving was thought to be a healthful activity and relaxing pastime. The silhouette of the new grand hotel, the Grove Park Inn, can be seen in the background across the golf course. (RFP, Emory.)

KATHLEEN AND JANE WITH NANNY. Thomas Raoul's daughters stand on the steps of their next home, Milfoil Cottage, with their nanny. Servants were provided rooms in many of the cottages, and a servants' building was situated behind The Manor. Others would commute from their own homes; some traveled with their employers. (JRBP, Emory.)

HORSE SHOW COMPETITION. Thomas Raoul was a founder of the Asheville Horse Show Association and served as a longtime president. Kathleen Doyle Lorillard (above), Helen Raoul's sister, competed in various events. She spent winters in Asheville, where she raised a number of ribbon-winning horses. Another ribbon winner was Edith Vanderbilt, whose husband, George, awarded cups at the Asheville Horse Show in Riverside Park. Mary Olmsted, wife of Frederick Law Olmsted, came as their guest. Alice Roosevelt Longworth wrote in response to an article on the 1903 Asheville show, "I was one of those in 'an enormous picture hat' with which I was rather smugly pleased!" The car jumping (below) was not known to be a typical event. Kathleen's uncle, Pierre Lorillard's horse, Iroquois, was the first American-bred horse to win the English Derby. (JRBP, Emory.)

ASHEVILLE HORSE SHOW. Parking spaces at Riverside Park were reserved for guests of The Manor. From left to right in the carriages are Beeckman "Dick" Lorillard, unidentified, Anna Doyle, a Mrs. Steele, a Mrs. Bennett, Kathleen Lorillard, Dr. Rodney Swope (All Souls Church), unidentified, unidentified boy, four unidentified passengers in back of carriage on right, Jack Frost, Mrs. Cam Waddell, Mrs. Henri Berger, Cameron Waddell, and three unidentified women. Dr. Cheesborough's eight-year-old son John is at lower left. The rest are unidentified. (JRBP, Emory.)

STEREOSCOPIC CARD OF THEODORE ROOSEVELT IN COURT SQUARE. Thomas Raoul attended the president's speech given in downtown Asheville in 1902. "The government is us; we are the government, you and I," Roosevelt told the crowd. He stayed at the Battery Park Hotel and visited Biltmore House. (NCC, Pack.)

WRITING FROM BREEZEMONT. Eleanore Miles sits at a worktable at Breezemont. Her father, Herbert Miles's poem, "Asheville, Queen of the Land of the Sky," begins: "Viewed from Breezemont the day is done; Shimmers a city of dreams—of air." It won a local newspaper contest. Miles's poem about the war, "1918," was published in the *New York Times*. (RSSR.)

HULBURD MILES AT BREEZEMONT. The youngest Miles child, Hulburd, showed his patriotism in the garden at Breezemont while his older brother, Edward, was serving in World War I. In a two-week battle, Edward's Ambulance Corps carried 1,771 wounded "through shellfire, almost all of the time . . . and in the dark, and by the dead . . . and dodging shell holes. And that awful gas." Some of Edward's letters to the Miles family from France were shared in newspapers. (RSSR.)

CORNELIA VANDERBILT CECIL'S FLOWER GIRL. Great excitement surrounded the 1924 wedding event of the Vanderbilts' daughter Cornelia to John F.A. Cecil. Thomas and Helen Raoul's daughter Jane (above, second from left) had the role of flower girl. Although Cornelia was 15 years older than Jane, "they all went around together." The wedding took place in the orange blossom–adorned All Souls Church, followed with a reception for 1,000 at the Biltmore House. The wedding party reassembled in Biltmore's Tapestry Gallery (below). Jane later spoke about the protective kneepads her mother required her to wear prior to the wedding to prevent scrapes. (Both, NCC, Pack.)

OUT-OF-DOOR THEATER. Louise A. Collins of Montford performed in Albemarle Park along with a classic, English-style repertory company that gave outdoor performances. The Ben Greet Players toured Great Britain and the United States to perform Shakespeare's plays. (NCC, Pack.)

CHILDREN'S OUTDOOR THEATER. The children perform *Alice in Wonderland* before an audience near the Clubhouse's tennis courts. There were always children in Albemarle Park, and cottages were promoted as being "ideal for family groups, or families with children—babies and their attendants. For even babies are welcome in this garden home." Sandboxes, rings and swings, and a flying trapeze were provided. (JRBP, Emory.)

COSTUMES ON STAGE. Children are grouped on the stage of The Manor's ballroom, possibly for a Halloween costume contest. Jane Raoul is front and center (dark vest). The stage in the 1903 wing was used for music and theatrical performances, both for the resort and the community. (JRBP, Emory.)

NEW YEAR'S EVE, 1914. The Manor's ballroom was a social center for Asheville. Alice Thomas Connally, of Fernihurst, gave this New Year's Eve party in 1914. Her daughter Alice Kerr Connally resided in Shamrock Cottage after marrying Dr. Thomas Patton Cheesborough. (NCC, Pack.)

LADIES' PARLOR. The second floor of The Manor contained the Ladies' Parlor. Floral swag wall decorations and breezy curtains adorning large windows offered views of the distant mountains and made for a more private space than the public rooms on the main floor. (APMGA.)

LOUISE COLLINS AS CELIA. The 1916 Shakespeare pageant billed Collins in the role of Celia in Shakespeare's *As You Like It*. Her husband, Willis, was an event promoter, musician, writer, and president of Biltmore Wheat Hearts Cereal Company. (NCC, Pack.)

THOMAS WOLFE'S PAGEANT. Thomas Wolfe (right) performed in a pageant with his North State Finishing School to commemorate the tercentenary of Shakespeare's death in 1916. Wolfe later recounted the event in *Look Homeward, Angel*: "The pageant was performed on the embowered lawns of The Manor House." Wolfe played Prince Hal but wrote about being embarrassed by his ill-fitting costume. The *Asheville Citizen* reported that the pageant had everything: "Artistic costumes, beautiful girls, wonderful interpretation of a master's lines and a natural stage setting that would be hard to surpass in America, if not the world." (Right, NCC, Pack; below, State Archives.)

DELIA MILES IN BREEZEMONT'S SUNROOM.
Breezemont's sunroom overlooks the
swimming pool and a wooded landscape.
Here, Delia Hulburd Gallup Miles,
Herbert's wife, reads in a wide-armed
wicker rocker on an Indian rug near
the terrace. She was the daughter of
a prominent Chicago lawyer. Herbert
Miles wrote that they came to Asheville
"for a milder climate of higher altitude;
she having developed a trouble resulting
in a permanent bronchitis." (RSSR.)

SWIMMING POOL AT BREEZEMONT. One of
the earliest in-ground concrete swimming
pools was constructed for the Miles family
at Breezemont. It was assembled when
few people could swim and is small by
today's standards. Miles was the largest
investor in the company that built Lake
Lure, where he constructed its first
lake house, Breezy Hollow. (RSSR.)

MILES AND JACKSON WEDDING, 1924. Herbert Miles's daughter Marjorie Chipman Miles married Winston Jerome Jackson at Breezemont. Winston was the engineer for his brother's neo-Gothic L.B. Jackson Building on Asheville's Pack Square. Built in the same year as this wedding, it was the first skyscraper in Western North Carolina. (RSSR.)

SAUNDERS FAMILY AT BREEZEMONT. Dr. Saunders, Asheville's first orthopedic surgeon, acquired Breezemont in 1944 from Herbert Miles. He created elaborate model train villages that occupied much of the large basement. His children often enjoyed long horseback rides over dirt roads and trails on Sunset Mountain. In 1936, Dr. Saunders had treated F. Scott Fitzgerald's dislocated shoulder for four months in Asheville, and they continued correspondence. (RSSR.)

CLEMENS SANDRESKY AND NINA SIMONE, 1948. Nina Simone's classical music education was rooted in Milfoil Cottage. Clemens Sandresky (above) had an apartment and music studio in Milfoil from 1946 to 1952. He also taught at Asheville-Biltmore College and was organist-choir director at All Souls Church before later becoming dean of Salem College's School of Music for 34 years. Nina, originally named Eunice Waymon, of Tryon, North Carolina, attended Asheville's Allen School for Girls and would walk to Albemarle Park for her private lessons with Sandresky. In the spring of 1948, Nina (seen left at school at age 17) performed a recital inside Milfoil, and "her people"—family and friends—listened from the lawn through open windows. Asheville's classical pianist, Grace Potter Carroll, was enthusiastic about the performance, and money was raised in Tryon to send Simone to Juilliard. Simone later wrote, "Bach made me dedicate my life to music." (Both, NSP.)

"My Day" by Eleanor Roosevelt. Roosevelt's visit to Asheville on November 29, 1956, was to give an evening speech on the United Nations, and she would only speak to an integrated audience. She wrote in her "My Day" newspaper column, "We stayed in a very pleasant hotel called The Manor . . . It was very comfortable and an open fire in my room made it look hospitable for the newspaper people who came in." Clark Eichelberger, executive director of the American Association of the United Nations, later wrote, "We had set up a big public meeting, a luncheon at the old Manor on Charlotte Street, which at that time was quite an elegant place still and in the afternoon she had interviews with people, and then that night we had a public meeting, a large one, set up for the YWCA." The 2:00 p.m. to 4:00 p.m. forum was for all interested people who wanted a discussion about the United Nations program. (Franklin D. Roosevelt Presidential Library.)

GRACE KELLY FILMING THE SWAN. Grace Kelly, Louis Jordan, Alec Guiness, Agnes Moorehead, and Leo Carroll stayed for three weeks at The Manor in 1955. Biltmore House became the film's Austrian palace in Kelly's final film, just before she became royalty in real life. Grace Kelly sent a postcard of The Manor to Louella Parsons with an X marking her room, reading, "Asheville is a fabulous town. It's an unbelievably magnificent place." (EMB, Ramsey.)

THE LAST OF THE MOHICANS SET. The 1992 film starring Daniel Day-Lewis used The Manor as the location to represent British headquarters at Albany, New York. Set designers temporarily reworked the facade to represent Colonial architecture. The Manor was in poor condition at the time, and the film helped bring some well-needed repairs specified by the Preservation Society of Asheville and Buncombe County. (APMGA.)

Eight

CHARLOTTE STREET AND ENVIRONS

Once characterized as "the ragged end of nowhere" by Thomas Raoul in 1897 when he arrived to begin work on Albemarle Park, Charlotte Street today is a bustling neighborhood corridor, and the area now claims the largest concentration of historic districts in Asheville.

After the Civil War, as the population of Asheville expanded with the arrival of the railroad in 1880, growth along Charlotte Street followed. Moving north along the corridor closest to town is the Chestnut Hill neighborhood. Coinciding with the railroad boom period, it was laid out in a typical grid pattern and was comprised primarily of single-family residences whose architecture reflected the growing cosmopolitan character of the city. The works of James Albert Tennent and Richard Sharp Smith are well represented in the district; both men were involved with the Albemarle Park development.

Moving north along the corridor and just past Albemarle Park is the Grove Park neighborhood, designed and developed by E.W. Grove, with assistance from Chauncey Beadle, nurseryman and later superintendent of the Biltmore Estate. Started in 1908, it is known for its curvilinear streets, eclectic architectural mix, and naturalistic landscaping. Continuing up Charlotte Street is Proximity Park, a streetcar suburb platted in 1907 on the site of a former golf course.

At the end of Charlotte Street on a sloping site overlooking the golf course currently operated by the Grove Park Inn is the small community of Sunset Terrace, its six cottages nestled into the hillside. Sunset Terrace was the vision of Rose Mary Byrne, who purchased the two-acre tract from Thomas Raoul for her development. The cottages were the work of local architect Charles N. Parker; his brother Harry L. Parker, an engineer, laid out the streets and landscaping. Though not intended as a resort, Byrne was apparently inspired by her stay in Milfoil Cottage, and the picturesque style of Albemarle Park influenced her vision for Sunset Terrace.

Trolley lines once provided access to Sunset Mountain from Charlotte Street. Sunset Mountain, touted in early tourism brochures for its charms and magnificent views, also served as a gateway to the Great Craggy Mountains beyond.

THE PARKER HOME AT CAMP PATTON. The Charlotte Street area was the site of a Civil War encampment and drill grounds for Confederate and Union troops before Thomas Walton Patton, mayor of Asheville (1893–1895), built his home on the site in 1868. The Patton family was very influential in Asheville and hosted a meeting here that led to the formation of the North Carolina Equal Suffrage Association. (NCC, Pack.)

CHARLOTTE STREET PHARMACY, AROUND 1920. The community pharmacy was located on the first level of this striking three-story brick building at the southwest corner of Charlotte and East Chestnut Streets. The Charlotte apartments occupied the two floors above. The apartment entrance is visible on the far left of the photograph. (EMB, Ramsey.)

GROVE PARK OFFICE. This small, rustic English cottage, designed by R.S. Smith and built as a real estate office for E.W. Grove in speculation of lot sales for his Grove Park subdivision on the Kimberly farm tract, later served as the Asheville Art Museum. At the time of its construction, around 1903, Charlotte Street ended at The Manor and a dirt track extended from there northward through the Kimberly farm pastures. (NCC, Pack.)

WOMAN BY FOUNTAIN AT GROVE PARK. A small park surrounds the former office of E.W. Grove on Charlotte Street. The concrete fountain is now a planting bed. The Charlotte Street entrance with its rough ashlar walls, beehive posts, and covered benches remains intact. St. Mary's Church, designed by R.S. Smith, is visible in the background. (NCC, Pack.)

111

STREET RAILWAY SYSTEM. Asheville was a leader in the development of streetcars, being the second city in the country with service, only behind Richmond, Virginia. The Street Railway Company was formed in 1886, and electric trolley service began in 1889. The Charlotte Street line passed by the gatehouse at Albemarle Park as it made its way from the public square (Pack Square) downtown to the terminus at the end of Charlotte Street. In 1891, a two-and-a-half-mile steam dummy line operated by the Asheville & Craggy Mountain Railway Company opened, connecting Charlotte Street to Sunset Mountain. Richard S. Howland, who arrived on the scene in 1899, bought the Asheville & Craggy Mountain Railway in 1900 and began construction of Overlook Park. (Above, EMB, Ramsey; below, NCC, Pack.)

DOLOBRAN, AROUND 1905. The home of Richard S. Howland, one of the first on Sunset Drive, was destroyed by fire in 1914. Howland, former editor of the *Providence Journal* in Providence, Rhode Island, arrived in Asheville in 1899, where he later purchased the *Asheville Citizen*. He was heavily involved in street railway development in Asheville and lived in Albemarle Park during construction of his house. (NCC, Pack.)

Asheville, N. C. Overlook Park.

OVERLOOK PARK. Across America, railway companies promoted suburban parks and recreation venues as supplemental revenue for their trolley systems. Howland's short-lived Overlook Park on Sunset Mountain was one such venture. Despite a dancing pavilion, shown here at right, and other amenities, the park was closed by August 1903, after just two years. It reopened again in 1909 for a brief stint. (NCC, Pack.)

PROXIMITY PARK. In 1899, this area was the site of a five-hole golf course for the Swannanoa Golf and Country Club and the golf club station, which was the departure point for the trolley to Overlook Park. The property was purchased in 1906 by the Proximity Park Company for development as a streetcar suburb. The Arts and Crafts style was popular in the initial development of the neighborhood, followed by period revival architecture in the 1920s. (NCC, Pack.)

SEELY'S CASTLE. Also known as Overlook, this residence is prominently sited on the crest of Sunset Mountain. It is a castellated stone mansion in the English Gothic style. Built between 1914 and 1917, it was conceived by Fred Loring Seely for his residence and designed with assistance from G.W. McKibbin. The structure is located on the former site of Overlook Park. Asheville-Biltmore College was located here after Seely's death. (NCC, Pack.)

TROLLEY ON MACON AVENUE, AROUND 1900. Before hauling passengers, the trolleys hauled stone from the Sunset Mountain quarry to a freight station on College Street for building roads in Asheville. Thomas Raoul worked as a foreman for Howland's company and supervised the paving of Charlotte and Chestnut Streets as well as the re-laying of the streetcar line. Asheville was the first city in the country to utilize an electric trolley line for building macadam roads. (NCC, Pack.)

HORSESHOE CURVE ON SUNSET MOUNTAIN. Originally the location of the trolley switchback, the tracks were re-laid, forming the curve in 1907. After the tracks were removed by E.W. Grove in 1911, truck trains used the road to haul wagons of boulders for construction of the Grove Park Inn. The Pleasant Knob trailhead, visible on the bottom left, led to an overlook with views of the Beaverdam Valley. (NCC, Pack.)

115

RAMBLER COTTAGE, SUNSET TERRACE, AROUND 1915. Rose Mary Byrne worked with Charles Parker, architect of the Grove Arcade, to design six cottages tucked naturally into the landscape at the end of Charlotte Street, overlooking the golf course. She lived for a while with her mother at Milfoil Cottage during the construction of her home and was active in the community. (NCC, Pack.)

ROSE MARY BYRNE IN ALASKA, 1919. Asheville's therapeutic climate attracted Rose Mary Byrne, who arrived in 1906 from Brooklyn, New York, with her mother after the death of her father and the loss of 11 siblings to tuberculosis. Resorts such as The Manor and Cottages and the benefits of Asheville's clear mountain air were routinely advertised in the *Brooklyn Daily Eagle*. (NCC, Pack.)

The Manor, Asheville, N. C.

TRANSFORMATION OF CHARLOTTE STREET. These two images of The Manor from Charlotte Street show the transformation of the streetscape from the trolley era to the automobile era. In the above photograph, a bench outside of the Lodge awaits a trolley passenger, while below, the 1940s-era traffic signal awaits an automobile. (Above, RSSR; below, NCC, Pack.)

RATTLESNAKE LODGE. This log structure, built in 1901, was the summer home of Dr. Chase Ambler, who was heavily involved in the creation of the Great Smoky Mountains National Park. The property is now part of the Blue Ridge Parkway, and trails built by Dr. Ambler are part of the Mountains-to-Sea Trail. Loring Raoul was a frequent visitor here. The Lodge burned in 1925. (NCC, Pack.)

NEW WINYAH SANATORIUM. The original Winyah Sanatorium opened in 1888 on Furman Street and was operated by scientist and pulmonary specialist Dr. Karl Von Ruck. Born in Turkey to German parents in 1849, he came to Asheville in 1886. In 1900, Von Ruck constructed this building on Spears Avenue before purchasing land at the foot of Sunset Mountain in 1904, where he lived until his death in 1922. (NCC, Pack.)

Nine

A LEGACY UNFOLDS

After the death of William Greene Raoul in 1913, the family decided that Albemarle Park needed to operate on a more profitable basis. An addition was made to The Manor, and the enterprise continued to operate successfully through 1920. Although previously not interested in purchasing the property, E.W. Grove had a change of heart and purchased The Manor in 1920 for twice what the Raouls had been willing to sell for in 1913. At about the same time, the trustees of the Vanderbilt estate had decided to sell off 1,500 acres of the Biltmore Estate to create a new residential park centered on a country club and golf course. This new development became the Town of Biltmore Forest, charted in 1923, with Thomas serving as president. Although Thomas never fully recovered from tuberculosis, he continued to lead a full and active life, serving the community until his death in 1953.

Albemarle Park was designated as a National Register Historic District in 1977 and as a local historic district in 1989. While many of the cottages have been remodeled, only Larkspur Cottage has been altered substantially. With the exception of a few garages, including the public garage near Charlotte Street and the stable behind Clio and Galax, all of the significant original structures remain. Because of this, the community retains a high degree of integrity and conveys that feeling to the visitor. The landscape has been altered somewhat by the needs of cars, which have replaced the horses and carriages. Many plantings have reached maturity or have been overtaken with exotic invasive species and are in need of restoration, but the landscape generally retains its essential character.

In an effort to promote the preservation of Albemarle Park in the 1980s, Rich Mathews, working with the Preservation Society of Asheville and Buncombe County, captured the spirit of the preservation effort thusly: "It's part of our soul, an example of our potential as a community, connecting us to our past and those spirited few who invigorated Asheville in the 1880s and 1890s with their grand aspirations."

THOMAS RAOUL AT BILTMORE ESTATE COMPANY OFFICE, AROUND 1920. This was the original office of the Biltmore Estate Company, located on Hendersonville Road. The company was formed by Thomas Raoul, along with Burnham S. Cogburn, Junius Green Adams, and William A. Knight in cooperation with Edith Vanderbilt. This structure served as the general administrative and sales office until the new office was completed in 1923. (JRBP, Emory.)

RAOULWOOD, AROUND 1924. This was Thomas Raoul's home in Biltmore Forest. While living here after the sale of Milfoil Cottage until his death in 1953, he served as president of the Biltmore Forest Company and as treasurer and clerk of the Town of Biltmore Forest. According to his daughter Jane, Thomas took all of the town's concerns personally and was loved and respected by all those who worked with him. Jane and her family continued living in Raoulwood until the late 2000s. (RFP, Emory.)

PLAYHOUSE IN BILTMORE FOREST, AROUND 1924. Kathleen Raoul and Jane Raoul Bingham pose on the front porch of their log cabin playhouse before their own house in Biltmore Forest was completed. They were disappointed to learn that there would be no farm animals at their new home and missed their friends from The Manor's grounds and the children of visiting guests. (TBF.)

THOMAS RAOUL SCULPTURE. This sculpture of a young Thomas is the work of Alexander Stirling Calder, a prominent sculptor and teacher from Philadelphia, Pennsylvania, whose works include the *Swann Memorial Fountain* in Philadelphia and the *Italian Barge* at Vizcaya in Miami. He may have met Thomas in Arizona, where both went to recover from tuberculosis in 1906. (RFP, Emory.)

THE AUDITORIUM. The Asheville Auditorium, located at Haywood and Flint Streets, opened with a production of the Burlesque Circus in 1902. Thomas Raoul helped raise funds for the facility while serving on the Asheville Board of Trade. The original structure burned in 1903 and was rebuilt in 1904. Sarah Bernhardt, Harry Houdini, and Will Rogers were among the entertainers who performed there before it was condemned by the city in the mid-1930s. (NCC, Pack.)

THE PEN AND PLATE CLUB. Thomas Raoul was a member of this club, which was devoted to literary discussion and was started in 1904 by a group of seven men, including Dr. Rodney Swope. George Vanderbilt recruited Swope from Wheeling, West Virginia, to serve as the first rector of All Souls Episcopal Church in 1897. (NCC, Pack.)

HERBERT DE LA HAYE MILES (1866–1958). Miles leased the Smith-McDowell House in 1913, after retiring to Asheville from Chicago and before commissioning Richard Sharp Smith to design Breezemont, his family home in Albemarle Park. Miles went on to have a lasting business and civic impact. Inspired by his extensive world travels, he was responsible for remodeling the Asheville Club, giving it an Italianate exterior and renaming it the Miles Building. In 1923, he was involved in the construction of the George Vanderbilt Hotel, a sister hotel to the new Battery Park Hotel; as president of the Vanderbilt Hotel Corporation, he donated property adjacent to the hotel for the new city auditorium. Miles was integral in establishing Pritchard Park by helping to push a bill through the US Congress to convey the old post office, located on the site, to the City of Asheville. Although Miles's chief interests were business, real estate, and cultural and civic works, he also took pleasure in publishing two books of his own poetry. (RSSR.)

GROVE PARK INN. The spectacular Grove Park Inn, a venture conceived by Edwin Wiley Grove, a pharmacist turned real estate developer, was completed in 1913. Originally from Tennessee, Grove made his fortune selling Tasteless Chill Tonic, a bottled form of quinine without the bitter taste. Arriving in Asheville in 1897, he became caught up in the real estate boom and began purchasing property. In partnership with his son-in-law, Fred Loring Seely, they designed the Grove Park Inn. Inspired by the Rustic-style Old Faithful Inn at Yellowstone National Park, Grove and Seely worked with Atlanta-based architectural engineer G.W. McKibbin to translate their concepts into reality. About this time, Thomas Raoul began to loose interest in running The Manor and attempted to sell to Grove. Although not interested at the time, Grove eventually purchased the Albemarle Park Company seven years later in 1920. (Both, NCC, Pack.)

ROCKING CHAIR PORCH AT GROVE PARK INN. The inn, built in less than a year with a crew of 400, is known for its expansive porches and scenic views. Most of the furnishing for the Grove Park Inn came from White Furniture of Mebane, North Carolina, when orders from the Roycrofters of East Aurora, New York, a well-known community of designers and manufacturers of Arts and Crafts–style furniture, were unable to fill the order on time. (NCC, Pack.)

STONE FIREPLACE AT GROVE PARK INN. The massive, rough-cut granite boulders, some weighing up to 10,000 pounds, used for the walls, chimneys, and the enormous lobby fireplaces were quarried from Sunset Mountain. In the delivery of his keynote address to 400 of the most distinguished men of the South, Secretary of State William Jennings Bryan proclaimed that the Grove Park Inn "was built for the ages." (NCC, Pack.)

GREAT SMOKY MOUNTAINS NATIONAL PARK. Thomas Raoul was appointed by the governor in 1933 to the North Carolina Park Commission, where he served for 14 years. As the federal government did not provide funding for land acquisition, park commissions in North Carolina and Tennessee were charged with raising the funds. Construction of the park began in 1931, but land acquisition continued until 1940, when Franklin D. Roosevelt officially dedicated the park. (State Archives of North Carolina.)

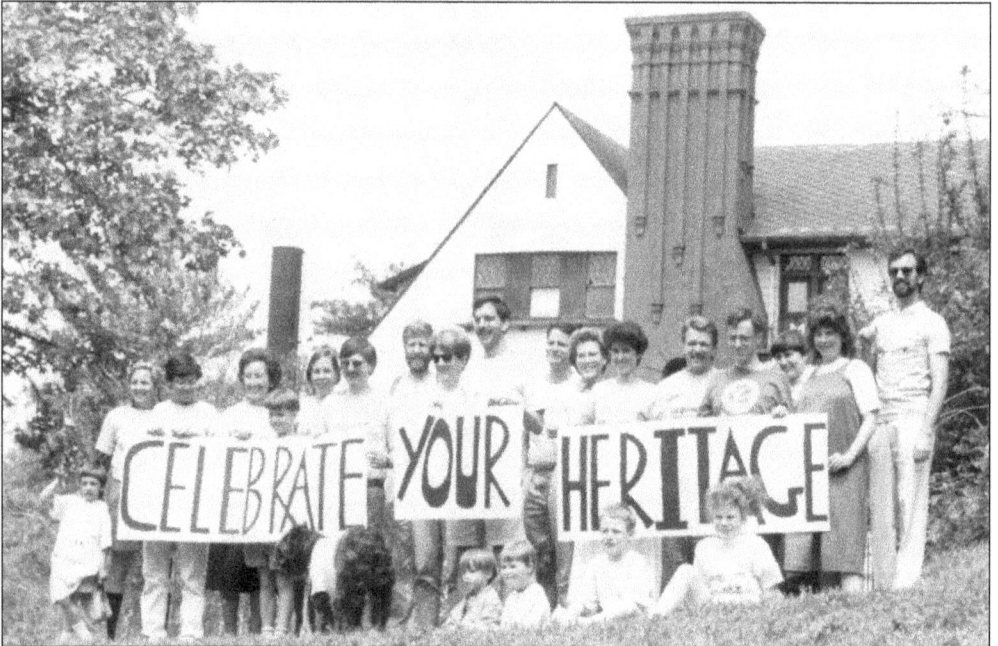

PRESERVATION OF THE MANOR. The Preservation Society of Asheville and Buncombe County spearheaded an effort to save The Manor from demolition in 1989 through a successful program designed to preserve distressed properties. The Manor was purchased by the organization and then resold with protective covenants, resulting in its preservation and rehabilitation for residential use as an apartment building. Leslie and Associates, Inc., currently owns and operates The Manor Inn Apartments. (PS.)

RETAINING WALL AT CHEROKEE ROAD AND SUNSET DRIVE. Rebuilt in the summer of 2013, the original retaining wall was designed by Samuel Parsons and built by Thomas Raoul in 1901. After handling storm-water runoff from Sunset Mountain for more than 100 years, the wall had been compromised due to a crack in the original tile drainage pipe, and stones were falling into the ravine. The City of Asheville contracted with Baker Engineering and Mathews Architecture on the engineering and design; Buchanan and Sons, Inc., served as general contractor. Masons with Independent Stoneworks carefully halved the original stone, identified as metagraywacke, and used the resultant stone faces as a veneer, covering the modern concrete retaining wall beneath. The Historic Resources Commission of Asheville and Buncombe County (HRC) reviewed the proposed plans for the new wall, and HRC director Stacy Merten worked closely with city engineer Brian Estes overseeing the construction. (Both, Brian Estes.)

Visit us at
arcadiapublishing.com

www.ingramcontent.com/pod-product-compliance
Lightning Source LLC
Chambersburg PA
CBHW080554110426
42813CB00006B/1302